Marie Curie

And the Science of Radioactivity

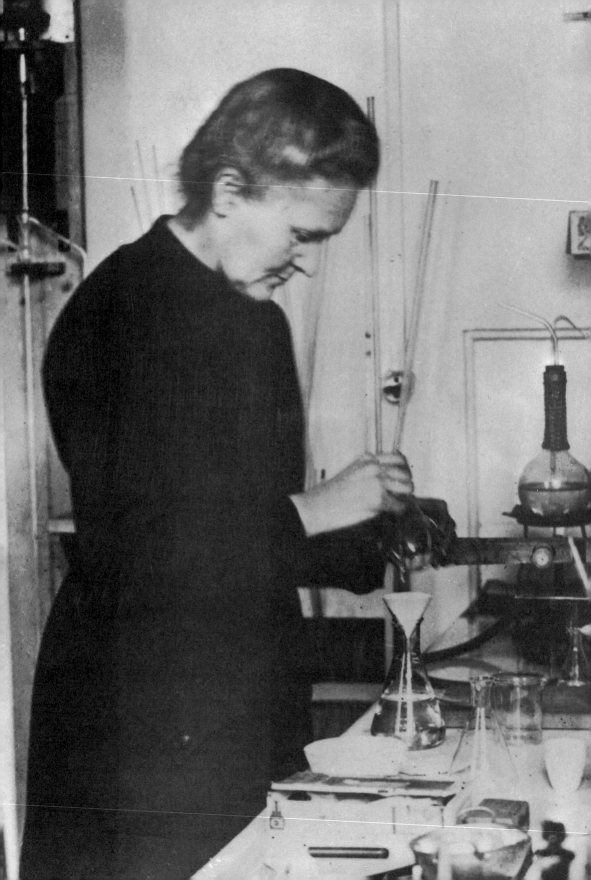

Owen Gingerich
General Editor

Marie Curie

And the Science of Radioactivity

Naomi Pasachoff

Oxford University Press
New York • Oxford

To my mother, Anna Jacobson Schwartz,
a role model for daughters and granddaughters

Oxford University Press

Oxford   New York
Athens Auckland Bangkok Bombay
Calcutta Cape Town Dar es Salaam Delhi
Florence Hong Kong Istanbul Karachi
Kuala Lumpur Madras Madrid Melbourne
Mexico City Nairobi Paris Singapore
Taipei Tokyo Toronto
and associated companies in
Berlin   Ibadan

Copyright © 1996 by Naomi Pasachoff
Published by Oxford University Press, Inc.,
198 Madison Avenue, New York, New York 10016

Design: Design Oasis
Layout: Leonard Levitsky
Picture research: Lisa Kirchner

Library of Congress Cataloging-in-Publication Data
Pasachoff, Naomi
Marie Curie and the science of radioactivity / Naomi Pasachoff.
p.   cm. — (Oxford portraits in science)
Includes bibliographical references and index.
ISBN 0-19-509214-7 (library ed.)
1. Curie, Marie, 1867–1934—Juvenile literature. 2. Chemists—Poland—
Biography—Juvenile literature. [1. Curie, Marie, 1867–1934. 2. Chemists. 3.
Women—Biography.] I. Title. II. Series.
QD22.C8P38 1995
540'.92—dc20
[B]   95-13639
                                             CIP

9 8 7 6 5 4 3 2 1

Printed in the United States of America
on acid-free paper

Cover and frontispiece: Marie Curie in her laboratory, 1921.

Contents

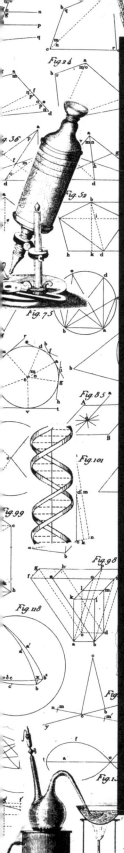

OXFORD PORTRAITS IN SCIENCE

Preface

In the Preface to her biography of her husband, Marie Curie wrote, "This narrative is, to be sure, neither complete nor perfect. I hope, nevertheless, that the picture it gives of Pierre Curie is not deformed, and that it will help to conserve his memory." Without claiming to have the same intimate knowledge of Marie Curie as she had of her subject, I would like nonetheless to express the same hope with regard to the total picture my book presents of her.

I am grateful to Marie Curie not only for her felicitous phrasing of the previous sentiment but also for inspiring the wording of each of this book's chapter titles, which are based on quotations from the *Autobiographical Notes* that follow her biography of her husband.

At age 16, Marie Sklodowska was a young woman with a first-rate intellect who was determined to receive an education.

"Preparation for Future Work"

It was hardly a run-of-the-mill blind date. The 26-year-old woman was, to be sure, blond. Some even thought her a beauty, with distinctive Slavic features and piercing, intelligent eyes. A faint foreign accent detectable in her French might reveal her Polish origins to a very attentive listener. The man, older by about a decade, had a touch of the dreamy poet in him. But what brought them together in Paris was not their lonely hearts but the pressing needs of scientific research.

The previous summer, the woman had finished first in her master's degree physics program at the Sorbonne, as the University of Paris was usually called. She would shortly finish second in the math program for a second master's degree at the same august Parisian university. Now she had been commissioned by the Society for the Encouragement of National Industry to do a study relating the magnetic properties of different types of steel to their chemical composition. She needed a place to work. A Polish physicist of her acquaintance, now professor at the University of Fribourg, was in Paris to give some lectures. When the woman mentioned to her countryman her need for laboratory space, he pondered her problem for a moment. Then he thought of a possible solution. His esteemed colleague Pierre Curie, who had done groundbreaking research on magnetic effects, was laboratory chief at the School of Industrial Physics and Chemistry in Paris. Perhaps, he suggested, Curie could find room for her to work on her commission at the school.

A graduate student meeting an established scientist in hope of finding research facilities—hardly the circumstances in which to expect romance. But her recollection of her first view of him, published nearly three decades later in the *Autobiographical Notes* she appended to her biography of him, would not be inappropriate coming from the mouth of a heroine of a romance novel: "Upon entering the room I perceived, standing framed by the French window opening on the balcony, a tall young man with auburn hair and large, limpid eyes. I noticed the grave and gentle expression of his face, as well as a certain abandon in his attitude, suggesting the dreamer absorbed in his reflections."

That meeting in the spring of 1894 did more than alter the lives of Pierre Curie and Marie Sklodowska. It brought together two people who, through their work, would produce fundamental changes in scientists' understanding of energy and matter, lead others to the discovery of new forces of nature, and change the course of history in the 20th century.

Although the turning point in Marie Curie's life did not come until she was past 25, her first quarter-century did not lack for drama. She was born in Warsaw on November 7, 1867, in a Poland whose struggle for political independence was to leave a distinct imprint on her. Once a proud empire, Poland over the centuries had weakened and declined. Toward the end of the 1700s, Austria, Prussia, and Russia began to take parts of Poland for themselves until, by 1795, it no longer existed as a separate country. Polish patriots attempted several revolts to remove the foreign oppressors, but none succeeded. Warsaw, where Marie's family lived, was in the part of Poland under the control of the Russian emperor, or czar.

Czarist Russia was particularly brutal in its attempts to obliterate the Polish national spirit. An uprising in 1863 resulted not only in the public hanging in Warsaw of the revolt's leaders but also in a vigorous attempt to wipe out Polish culture. Russian officials were appointed to replace Polish ones. The educational system was placed under central Russian control. Attempts to teach Polish history, language, or literature became punishable offenses. Even very young Polish children knew that if an informer overheard them speaking Polish or uttering a patriotic sentiment they might be endangering themselves and their families. Not surprisingly, the Russian attempt to suppress Polish national feeling had the opposite effect; it heightened the devotion of Poles to their country and culture.

A musician and educator, Marie Sklodowska's mother died of tuberculosis when her youngest daughter was 10 years old.

Marie Sklodowska was deeply affected by these political pressures in at least three ways: as the daughter of teachers, as a student, and as a friend. Upon the birth of Marie, the fifth child in the family, her mother resigned her position as head of a school where the family had made their home. Her father took a new position as a teacher of mathematics and physics at a boys' high school. As "under-inspector"—the highest administrative position a Pole could have in a school—he received both a higher salary and living quarters for the family. But he was under the supervision of a Russian administrator, who found him lacking in pro-Russian sentiment. Eventually, his inability to mask his Polish national leanings led to his dismissal and to a series of successively lower teaching posts. With the decline in their economic situation, the Sklodowski family had to take in student boarders for a number of years. When Marie was only eight, her oldest sister caught typhus from one of the boarders and died.

The Russian-dominated educational system not only destroyed Marie's father's prospects, but it also inflicted humiliation and pain on her personally, as a student and as a friend. Marie's gifts as a student turned her, though the youngest child in the class, into the reluctant star pupil who was called upon whenever the Russian inspector made surprise visits to the school. On one occasion, when Marie was 10, the inspector put her through a sort of czarist catechism, asking her first to name all the czars and then to identify the current czar, Alexander II, as the ruler of Poland. According to her daughter Eve, Marie and her best friend celebrated the news of Alexander II's assassination four years later by dancing among the desks at school. She felt no more warmly toward his successor, Alexander III. A brother of one of her classmates was hanged for his involvement in a plot against the czar, and Marie and her sisters spent a night by the side of the grieving girl. Despite her aversion to Russian domination, in June 1883 Marie had to shake the hand of the grandmaster of education in Russian Poland, who awarded her a gold medal upon her completion of high school.

Marie's early years were less than carefree, not only because of the political situation in Poland, but also because of a personal loss. Her mother contracted tuberculosis when Marie was 5 and died at the age of 42, before Marie turned 11. During that period of more than five years, Marie's mother made a conscious effort, for fear of spreading the disease, to refrain from hugging and kissing the children whom she adored. Marie and her siblings did not fully understand their mother's behavior and felt alienated from her. Having experienced in swift succession the deaths of her oldest sister and her mother, Marie, who had faithfully attended Catholic services with her mother, no longer found credible the idea of a loving God.

Despite their emotional losses and financial difficulties, the remaining members of the family—Professor Sklodowski, his son Joseph, and daughters Bronya, Hela, and Marie—drew ever more closely together. Throughout her life, the members of her family shared Marie's joys and successes and sustained her through times of crisis. Professor Sklodowski reproached himself throughout his life for losing the family savings in a bad investment, but his children remembered him for the

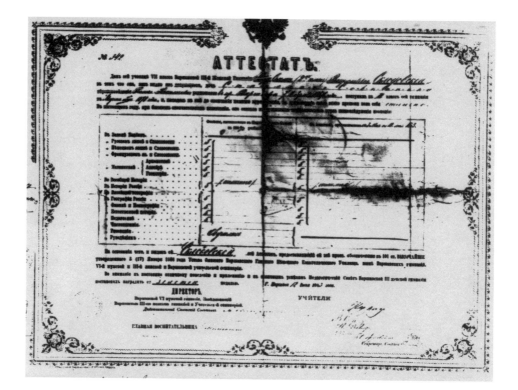

emotional and intellectual sustenance his home provided. They recalled, for example, the Saturday nights when their father read them world classics of literature and the family occasions that he commemorated with original poems.

Marie was able to develop a broad range of interests in her father's home, and in fact it was not until her 20s that she clearly defined her goals as a scientist. Still, according to her daughter Eve, even as a young child Marie was drawn to two particular items in the Sklodowski home: a precision barometer that her father occasionally regulated and cleaned in the presence of the children, and a glass case filled with scientific apparatus he had once used in physics classes but that now were permanently at home, following the Russian orders reducing the number of hours of science instruction in Polish schools.

All the Sklodowski children were eager to pursue advanced studies. Joseph, as a male, was permitted to study

Marie Sklodowska's secondary school diploma shows that she got top grades in every subject. Nevertheless, Marie found her attempts at further education blocked by the University of Warsaw's policy against admitting women.

medicine at the University of Warsaw. But that institution would not admit Polish women until 1915, although women students were accepted at universities in other European cities. Encouraged by a friend, Marie and Bronya attempted to circumvent the barriers the Russian system erected for Polish women by joining other young Poles in an illegal night school. The classes were held not in university buildings but rather in varying locations to avoid detection by the Russian authorities. As a result, the participants called the venture the "Floating University." In the Floating University, Marie was introduced to progressive currents of thought as well as to the latest developments in physics, chemistry, and physiology (the study of how living things function). The mission of the patriotic participants in the Floating University was to bring about Poland's eventual freedom by enlarging and strengthening its educated classes.

Realizing that the activities of the Floating University, admirable as they might be, were no substitute for a rigorous education at a major university, Bronya and Marie struck a bargain: Marie would stay in Poland and work as a private tutor, setting aside money that she would send to Bronya, who would study medicine in Paris. Then, as soon as she was able to return the favor, Bronya would help Marie realize her own academic goals. Thus, before she turned 17, Marie began giving private lessons, teaching a variety of subjects to the children of well-to-do families. After two years, she realized that she was not saving enough money both for Bronya's and her own expenses, and she took a job as a governess in the home of the owner of a beet-sugar factory. In Szczuki, the village where the family lived, about 100 miles (150 kilometers) north of Warsaw, there would be few things on which the young governess could fritter away her excellent salary of 500 rubles a year. Marie was to remain in this post for the next three years.

She took no summer vacation following her first half year of work in Szczuki. As a result, she met and fell in love with the family's oldest son, himself on vacation from agricultural engineering studies in Warsaw. Before his arrival on the scene, Marie had already determined that this was a family with sentiments similar to her own in some respects. When she asked her employer for permission to use some of her spare time to tutor the illiterate peasant children whose parents enabled the beet-sugar business to thrive, he not only agreed but also allowed his older daughter to assist Marie, even though he knew that the Russian authorities considered such clandestine teaching to be treason.

Before the son's return to school in the fall, the young couple had agreed to marry. But although Marie's employers were very fond of her, they had higher aspirations for their son than marriage to a penniless governess, and the young man lacked the courage to stand up to his parents. As uncomfortable as the situation must have been for Marie when the engagement was broken, she was able to put her responsibility to her sister above her personal feelings, and she fulfilled the rest of her three-year contract with the family.

Rather than dwell on her broken heart, Marie devoted her evenings, and occasionally the very early mornings, to studying. Initially, she followed her interests in all directions, reading sociology and literature along with physics and chemistry textbooks, and learning mathematics through an informal correspondence course her father conducted in his letters to her. She later wrote in her *Autobiographical Notes,* "during these years of isolated work, trying little by little to find my real preferences, I finally turned towards mathematics and physics, and resolutely undertook a serious preparation for future work." Her employer made the factory library available to her, and so impressed by her commitment was a chemist at the factory that he gave her 20 chemistry lessons. Still, as she wrote to her brother in October 1888, the lack of a laboratory in which she could experiment with the scientific knowledge she was gaining from books and lessons was a source of frustration: "I am learning chemistry from a book. You can imagine how little I get out of that, but what can I do, as I have no place to make experiments or do practical work?" Little did she guess that lack of satisfactory laboratory conditions was to be a source of distress for many years to come.

Looking back on her attempts at self-education during her years as a governess, Marie was to reflect on her habit of picking up books at random: "This method could not be greatly productive, yet it was not without results. I acquired the habit of independent work, and learned a few things which were to be of use later on."

For a year following Marie's return to Warsaw in 1889, she held another live-in position as a governess before returning to her father's home and to private tutoring. Professor Sklodowski's financial situation had improved during Marie's absence. As director of a reform school near Warsaw, he now earned enough to send a monthly stipend to Bronya in Paris.

In 1890, Professor Vladislav Sklodowski was photographed in Warsaw with his three grown daughters: Marie, Bronya, and Hela.

At Bronya's request, he deducted a fraction of the stipend and set it aside to repay Marie for the money she had been sending Bronya over the years.

Finally, it was decided that Marie should come to Paris in the fall of 1891, in time for the opening courses at the Sorbonne. She could live with Bronya and her new husband, Polish activist Casimir Dluski, whom Bronya had met in medical school.

In the remaining months in Warsaw, Marie made a determined effort to fill a gap in her education. Up until now she had not had any laboratory experience. The Russian authorities had eliminated practical exercises in science from the Polish curriculum. But one of Marie's cousins, Joseph Boguski, who had once been an assistant to the Russian chemist Dmitri Mendeleev, directed a laboratory with an intentionally misleading name, "Museum of Industry and Agriculture." What Russian would suspect that the purpose of the so-called museum was to train young Poles in science? Marie spent her evenings and Sundays there, occasionally in the company of her cousin or one of his colleagues who had studied with the German chemist Robert Bunsen. This colleague and his assistant were kind enough to respond to Marie's enthusiasm by giving her a crash course in chemistry in their spare time.

More often than not, however, Marie found herself alone in the "museum," after hours, attempting to carry out the experiments that were described in the physics and chemistry books she read. Try as she might to follow instructions carefully, her procedures did not always produce the results described in the texts. Although these early laboratory experiences often filled her with despair, they also taught her, as she later wrote, "that the way of progress is neither swift nor easy." Her first, difficult experiences in her cousin's laboratory strengthened her conviction that "experimental research in the fields of physics and chemistry" was precisely the activity to which she was best suited.

text continues on page 21

DMITRI IVANOVICH MENDELEEV AND THE PERIODIC TABLE OF THE ELEMENTS

D mitri Ivanovich Mendeleev (1834–1907) was a Russian chemist best known for organizing the elements into a "periodic table." In a periodic table, elements are arranged by name in rows and columns so that those that behave similarly appear at regular intervals, or periods. Elements are the basic, pure substances that, separately or in combination, make up everything around us. Just as all the words in the English language are made up of different combinations of 26 letters, so all things in the universe are made up of different combinations of about 110 different elements. An element is a substance composed of only one kind of atom that cannot be broken down into other substances by electricity, light, or heat. Ancient philosophers believed in the concept of elements, but they were wrong in identifying water, for example, as such a basic substance. Today it is common knowledge that by passing electricity through water we can break it down into two elements. Each molecule of water consists of two hydrogen atoms and one oxygen atom.

Elements have both physical and chemical properties. At room temperature, some elements are liquids; others are gases; still others are solids, which may be soft or hard, dull or shiny, metallic or non-metallic. All these characteristics are examples of physical properties. How easily or violently elements react with each other or, for example, with water or air, are examples of chemical properties. By Mendeleev's time, scientists recognized more than 60 elements. Today we know of at least 110 elements, about 90 of which occur in nature. The remaining elements are artificially made by scientists.

Before Mendeleev, chemists had many rules for combining different elements, but they had no overall understanding of how the elements were related to each other or why they exhibited certain chemical and physical properties. Nor did they know about the building blocks of atoms called electrons, protons, and neutrons. We now know that protons and neutrons are made out of quarks, so atoms are really made of quarks and electrons. It is the electrons that determine how elements combine with one another. But chemists in Mendeleev's time could determine the atomic weight of each element—that is, how many times heavier its atoms were compared to the mass of the hydrogen atom, the lightest known element.

Mendeleev created a table or chart that listed the known elements consecutively in ascending order of atomic weights. Mendeleev found a way of dividing the chart into horizontal rows that revealed a pattern. In laying out the elements in his first periodic table, Mendeleev had to leave some gaps so that the known elements would form a part of the pattern. Elements with similar chemical properties appeared at regular intervals—that is, periodically—in vertical columns on the table. Each row of the table was called a "period." By consulting the periodic table, scientists could for the first time see the chemical

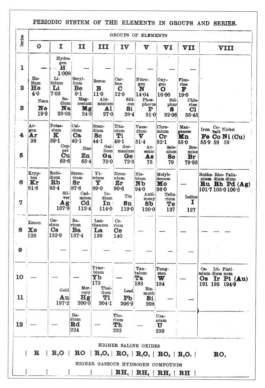

relationships among elements. Mendeleev predicted the properties of three as-yet-undiscovered elements that would fill the gaps in his table.

Mendeleev had discovered his periodic table gradually. In 1859 the Russian authorities sent Mendeleev to the University of Heidelberg for additional studies. In September 1860 he attended a German scientific conference. There he was exposed to the work of other chemists who had made advances in calculating atomic weights. The following year, Mendeleev returned to Russia, and in 1867 he was made professor of general chemistry at the University of St. Petersburg. Unable to find a satisfactory textbook, Mendeleev began to write his own. In his book, *The Principles of Chemistry,* Mendeleev worked out the periodic table to facilitate the classification of elements, providing a framework for modern chemical and physical theory. Mendeleev's textbook was translated into other languages and appeared in several editions. In the editions that followed Marie Curie's work

DMITRI IVANOVICH MENDELEEV AND THE PERIODIC TABLE OF THE ELEMENTS

continued from previous page

on radium, Mendeleev included a footnote referring to that work, noting that radium resembles barium and has an atomic weight between 223 and 225.

Like many new ideas, Mendeleev's periodic table was not instantly accepted by the entire scientific community. But within 20 years the predictive value of the table had become clear. The discovery of the elements gallium (in 1875), scandium (in 1879), and germanium (in 1886) filled in three gaps in Mendeleev's table, as he had predicted, and thus supported the theory underlying it. Each of the new elements displayed properties that accorded with those Mendeleev had predicted, based on the idea that elements in the same column have similar chemical properties.

Even as Mendeleev's periodic table began to win wide acceptance, it was clear that some problems arose from its arrangement of the elements in order of atomic weight. For example, the atomic weight of argon—a gas that does not react readily with other elements—would place it in the same group as lithium and sodium, two solids that are very chemically active. In 1913 a British physicist solved the problem by showing that an element's chemical properties are related more closely to its atomic number—the number of protons in the nucleus of each atom—than to its atomic weight, which is roughly equal to the total number of protons and neutrons. Since then the periodic table has been rearranged so that the elements are listed according to their atomic numbers. The success of Mendeleev's version of the periodic table was due to the fact that atomic weights generally increase in the same order as atomic numbers. Both original and current versions of the table depend on the fact that an atom has the same number of electrons (which are responsible for chemical properties) as protons. Today's periodic table is divided into 7 periods—the horizontal rows of different lengths—and 18 groups—vertical columns. The chemical properties of elements change gradually along a period. Elements in a group exhibit similar properties.

text continued from page 17

Finally, not without regrets at having to leave her father, brother, and sister behind in Warsaw, Marie set out for formal university studies in Paris in the autumn of 1891. As instructed by Bronya, she had sent ahead such things as a mattress, sheets, and towels to avoid having to spend money on them when she arrived. Also to save money, she traveled fourth class in Germany, the only country to offer this super economy fare. Since no dining services or seats were provided for fourth-class travelers, Marie brought with her not only sufficient food and reading for the trip but also a folding chair and a blanket. Her intention was to use a French university education to enable her to fulfill an ideal imbued in her by the Floating University. In her *Autobiographical Notes,* she summarized that ideal: "You cannot hope to build a better world without improving the individuals. To that end each of us must work for his own improvement, and at the same time share a general responsibility for all humanity, our particular duty being to aid those to whom we think we can be most useful." She could have no idea in 1891 exactly how, or how fully, she would live up to that ideal.

In Paris, and especially as a student at the Sorbonne, Marie Sklodowska found the intellectual freedom she had long sought.

"The Heroic Period"

It would have been easy for Marie to let herself be seduced by the freedom she found upon arriving in Paris in the autumn of 1891. Although she had lived away from home before, the remote village of Szczuki offered none of the temptations of the French capital. Paris, with its recently erected Eiffel Tower, its newly installed electric street lamps, and its few but impressive automobiles, was like nothing Marie had seen before. More important, for the first time she could read what she wanted and speak whatever language she wanted to speak without having to look fearfully over her shoulder. She might have been tempted to spend days on end in the numerous museums Paris had to offer, or her nights at its theaters and concert halls.

Marie could also have chosen to throw herself wholeheartedly into the small but active community of Polish exiles who lived in Paris. For some months, in fact, she found it hard to resist this temptation. Her sister and brother-in-law were very involved with the exile community, and her brother-in-law insisted on having her participate in every gathering. It was fashionable at the time for cultured people to stage tableaux vivants, where they would dress in costume on a small stage or in a drawing room and form a silent, motionless, living picture. In one such patriotic tableau, Marie, dressed in a red tunic, with her blond hair cascading over her shoulders, portrayed "Poland Breaking Her Bonds." When she described the evening and her role in it to her father, anticipating his approval, his return letter warned her of the possible consequences such behavior might have on her future career in Poland or on the lives of her relatives there. "Events such as concerts, balls, etc., are described by certain correspondents for newspapers, who mention names. It would be a great grief to me if your name were mentioned one day. This is why, in my previous letters, I have made a few criticisms, and have begged you to keep to yourself as much as possible."

Ultimately, however, it was not parental disapproval but her own internal sense of purpose that kept Marie on course. Her commitment to Polish independence had not diminished, but she understood that she was in Paris for a purpose: to complete her studies as thoroughly and efficiently as possible. The home of Bronya and Casimir Dluski was in what was then an outlying district of Paris—La Villette. The long commute to the Sorbonne—about an hour by horse-drawn bus—was wasting too much of Marie's time, and the carfare too much of her limited funds. So, with the help of the Dluskis, she moved closer to school, to the celebrated Latin Quarter, the colorful Paris neighborhood that continues to serve as home to students and artists. In a letter to her brother, Marie described her room as "little . . . very suitable, and nevertheless very cheap. In a quarter of an hour I can be in the chemistry laboratory, in 20 minutes at the Sorbonne." Marie's accommodations were indeed basic, but no more so than those of countless other poor university students. Unlike many others, however, Marie chose not to live with roommates. She had already seen how easy it was to let socializing interfere with work.

In one sense, Marie did indeed revel in the independence she found in Paris during her student years. As she described it years later, it was not a question of forgetting her goal by succumbing to the freedom to indulge herself. Rather, the newfound freedom to pursue science rigorously provided a strict focus for her existence: "This life, painful from certain points of view, had, for all that, a real charm for me. It gave me a very precious sense of liberty and independence . . . All my mind was centered on my studies, which especially at the beginning, were difficult."

If Marie had sensed during her years in Poland that her scientific preparation had been scattershot, she now found out just how accurate that assessment was. Not only had her French classmates benefited from a much more thorough

When she first got to Paris, Sklodowska socialized primarily with other Polish students, one of whom drew this portrait of her in 1892.

mathematical and scientific preparation, but they also had no trouble understanding the professors' rapid technical French. To compensate for the deficiencies in her background, Marie had to work especially hard. As she later recalled, "I divided my time between courses, experimental work, and study in the library. In the evening I worked in my room, sometimes very late into the night." She often chose to stay in the library until it closed at ten, because, unlike her own room, the library was heated in the winter and better ventilated in the summer. But rather than balk at the restraints that this academic self-discipline put on other aspects of her life, Marie took pleasure in the dedication to work alone. "All that I saw and learned that was new delighted me. It was like a new world opened to me, the world of science, which I was at last permitted to know in all liberty."

In her *Autobiographical Notes,* Marie noted that her brother-in-law dubbed her student years "the heroic period" of her life, by way of teasing her about her self-denial. In fact, some of the anecdotes about Marie from those years do have a tinge of the melodramatic about them. There was the time when, wanting to spend neither the money needed to buy food nor the time needed to prepare it, she fainted from hunger, and had to be brought to the Dluskis' home for a period of fattening up. There are the stories of how she kept warm at night during the frigid winter months by wearing every stitch of clothing she owned, even piling her few sticks of furniture on top of herself for additional warmth. But for Marie, her student years in Paris were memorable not for the privation she underwent but for the opportunity they afforded her at long last to devote herself to her studies. Overcoming the obstacles of her inadequate preparation, in 1893 Marie finished first in her class with the equivalent of a master's degree in physics, and in 1894 she finished in second place in mathematics. When, after completing the first degree, it was not clear that she could scrape together the money to study for the second degree, she was providentially awarded a scholarship, given each year to an outstanding Polish student for study abroad. The donors of the stipend were undoubtedly taken by surprise when, four years later, Marie returned to them from her first earnings the sum she had been granted, in order that the money be used to help some other poor Polish student.

Marie's meeting with Pierre Curie in the spring of 1894 brought together two kindred spirits. Pierre had been in love only once before, about 15 years earlier, but when the young woman died, he gave up on love altogether. He considered most women too frivolous, and resented what he saw as their attempts to distract men of science from serious work. But Marie was something else entirely. His first gift to her was neither flowers nor candy but a reprint of his most recent publication, "On Symmetry in Physical Phenomena: Symmetry of an Electric Field and of a Magnetic Field," which he inscribed to her "with the respect and friendship of the author." Because Marie shared his dedication to science, Pierre saw right away that this was a woman with whom he could share his life.

He was first to commit himself to the relationship, and it was Marie who continued for some months to harbor doubts. When she visited Poland for a vacation in the summer of 1894 after her triumph in the mathematics exam, she was not even

Already an established scientist, Pierre Curie courted Marie by presenting her with a personally inscribed copy of one of his articles on magnetism.

certain she would return to Paris. Her intention had always been to live in Poland after completing her education, and to seek a position doing scientific research in her native land. She was also concerned about making permanent what she had intended to be a temporary separation from her father. Pierre's ardent letters served their purpose, however, and at summer's end, Marie returned to Paris to resume experimental work in preparation for her doctorate. She worked in the laboratory of one of her professors, Gabriel Lippmann, who would go on to win the Nobel Prize for physics in 1908 for his work in producing the first color photographic plate.

Pierre and Marie were married in July 1895 in a simple civil ceremony attended by Marie's father and sister Hela, who had made the trip from Warsaw; Pierre's parents; and the Dluskis. Marie wore a simple outfit, a present from Bronya's mother-in-law, chosen for its practicality—Marie would be able to wear this dark blue garment for years to come in the laboratory. The marriage, according to Marie's later description, realized the goal of a "man who, without fortune himself, desired to share his life with that of a student also without fortune, whom he had met by chance." The newlyweds spent their honeymoon touring France on their new bicycles, a wedding gift from a cousin of Marie's.

The newly married Curies set off on their honeymoon: a bicycle tour of the French countryside.

As much as the couple enjoyed their wedding trip, and all the subsequent trips they would make through France on their bicycles, they were both what we would call workaholics, ever

eager to get back to serious work. Marie later recalled Pierre's expressing that impatience to resume productive research in remarks like "It seems to me a very long time since we have accomplished anything."

In fact, by the time of their marriage, Pierre had already accomplished a great deal, scientifically speaking. Together with his older brother Jacques, he had done important research on crystals—solids composed of atoms arranged in an orderly pattern. In 1880, when Pierre was only 21, he and Jacques discovered what is called the piezoelectric effect. The prefix piezo comes from the Greek word meaning "to press." Jacques and Pierre had discovered that when pressure is applied to certain crystals, they can generate voltage. The brothers also found that these same crystals become compressed under the influence of an electric field. Jacques and Pierre immediately put their discovery to use by designing a new device, the piezoelectric quartz electrometer, which could accurately measure very faint electric currents. The piezoelectric effect has since been used in a variety of practical devices, including microphones, electronic components, and quartz watches.

Jacques went on to become head lecturer in mineralogy at the University of Montpellier, and Pierre became director of laboratory work at the School of Industrial Physics and Chemistry (SIPC) in Paris, where he began his pioneering work on magnetism. Pierre studied the way in which certain materials undergo a marked change in their magnetic properties with a change in temperature. The temperature at which these changes take place is known as the Curie point, after Pierre's work. He also invented an extremely sensitive scientific balance, likewise named in his honor.

Pierre's scientific achievements won him the admiration of no less a figure than Great Britain's Lord Kelvin (1824–1907), one of the major physicists of the day, whose contributions in several fields helped shape the scientific thought of his era. Kelvin's opinion notwithstanding, however, Pierre's scientific contributions had not secured him an appropriate university position. His educational background was untraditional, and he did not have the support of influential backers. When Pierre was only a boy, his father, a physician, had sensed that Pierre's intelligence and personality would better flourish under private tutoring than ordinary schooling, and so Pierre received private instruction. Although he began university studies at the age of 16, and was awarded the equivalent of a master's degree at the age of 18, Pierre's financial situation kept him from continuing on toward his doctorate and forced him instead to become head of student laboratory work in physics at the Sorbonne. The fact that Pierre was able to conduct his own research in that position and later at the School of Industrial Physics and Chemistry was a measure of his own energy and commitment to science, for the laboratories placed at his disposal were not of the best quality.

For her entire life, Marie harbored a grudge against the French scientific establishment for failing to provide one of its most creative researchers with an appropriate laboratory facility. In *Pierre Curie,* her biography of her husband, Marie spoke bitterly of the work space available to him as chief of the laboratory at SIPC: ". . . he had to content himself with very little. He set up certain of his experiments in the rooms of his pupils when these were not in use. But more frequently he worked in an outside corridor running between a stairway and a laboratory." She also minced no words in describing Pierre's initial post at SIPC as a "small position," not proportionate to "his merits," with a very modest salary "comparable to that of a day laborer."

While Marie fully understood and respected the man who would become her husband, and recognized that "his independence of character" made it difficult for him to ask for what he deserved, she nonetheless insisted that Pierre write up his research on magnetism with a view to earning a much-deserved and very belated doctorate. He was awarded the degree in March 1895, a few months before their wedding. At about the same time, the director of SIPC, Paul

Pierre (upper right) and
Jacques Curie with their
parents. Like his
younger brother,
Jacques Curie was also
a research scientist.

Schützenberger, created expressly for Pierre a new chair of
physics. Unfortunately, the new position, while it brought
with it a higher salary, also increased Pierre's already demanding teaching responsibilities without providing any compensat-
ing improvement in laboratory facilities.

Marie spent the first year after their marriage preparing
for an examination that would qualify her to teach science to
young women. She passed the examination, first in her class,
in August 1896. She also continued her work on the commissioned study of the magnetic properties of steel. "Papa
Schütz," as the SIPC director was fondly called, permitted her
to work alongside Pierre in whatever "unused corner" he
might find at the school for his own research on crystals, and
she left Lippmann's laboratory to work with her husband. The

school offered no financial support for her research, but several metallurgical firms furnished her with free samples of steel. By the summer of 1897, she had successfully written up her research and received payment from the Society for the Encouragement of National Industry.

In September 1897, following another bicycle trip, the Curies' first child, Irène, was born. Pierre's father served as obstetrician. Pierre and Marie were immediately confronted by a problem that still worries dual-career couples today: how parents can best balance the demands of parenthood with those of their chosen professions, particularly when financial

The Curies' daughters, Irène and Eve, at ages eight and one. Pierre's father helped raise the girls.

resources are limited. According to Marie, Pierre "would not even think of" her giving up her scientific work just because she had become a mother: "Neither of us would contemplate abandoning what was so precious to both." Although up until now Marie had managed the household as well as her professional work, they now had to contemplate hiring help. However, a family tragedy worked to their advantage. Pierre's mother had died of breast cancer shortly after Irène's birth, and Pierre's father had retired and moved in with the Curies. Now the family moved into a small house with a garden on the rue Kellerman. Marie remained in charge of Irène's care, but while she was in the lab, the baby "was in the care of her grandfather, who loved her tenderly and whose own life was made brighter by her. So the close union of our family enabled me to meet my obligations." Pierre and Marie had neither time, nor money, nor energy for anything but work and family, but in spite of the hardships Marie always looked back fondly on these days of "quiet living," before their scientific achievements thrust them into a much larger world.

The Curies, with their laboratory assistant, measuring radioactivity in their laboratory with the piezoelectric quartz balance devised by Jacques and Pierre Curie in the 1880s.

"The Best and Happiest Years"

With childcare provided for her infant daughter and with her first research on magnetism in steel completed, Marie Curie began to look around for an appropriate topic for her doctoral research. At the time she began this undertaking, no woman anywhere in the world had yet been awarded a doctorate in science, although an unmarried German woman was well into her thesis research in electrochemistry.

To understand Marie's choice of topic, it is useful to know a little bit about two scientific discoveries that had been made a short time before. In 1895, the year of the Curies' marriage, the German physicist Wilhelm Roentgen (1845–1923) discovered a new kind of ray, which he called the X ray, with X standing for "unknown." For this Roentgen was awarded the first Nobel Prize for physics in 1901. Scientists around the world were immediately fascinated by X rays, which could travel through solid substances and produce photographs of people's bones. Only a few months after the discovery of X rays, the French physicist Henri Becquerel found, by accident, that a sample of uranium ore emitted rays that could fog a photographic plate even without exposure to light. Despite the presentation of his results to the French Academy of Sciences in

February 1896, few scientists—including Becquerel himself—paid much attention to these "Becquerel rays" or "uranium rays." The fascination with the previously discovered X rays continued to monopolize scientific attention.

Marie seized on Becquerel's neglected uranium rays for her doctoral topic. Although scientific curiosity played the major role, she later admitted that, because she would be studying a new phenomenon, she would not have to read a long bibliography of scientific articles as preparation for her work, and this was another consideration. She could begin her experimental work immediately.

First, however, she would have to find a laboratory. "Papa Schütz" gave her permission to use a storeroom at SIPC. Although the conditions in the damp, crowded room were far from ideal for carrying out sensitive experiments, at least she would not have to carry out her work in the school corridors.

This hurdle having been overcome, her next goal was to make careful measurements of the phenomenon that Becquerel had discovered. Using the electrometer designed by Pierre and his brother, she was able to make precise measurements of the very faint electric fields that uranium rays generated as they passed through the air. In order to make sure that her results were accurate, she repeated her experiments more than once. Her accomplishment was all the more commendable given the dampness of her laboratory, since moist air dissipates electric charges more readily than dry air.

Through repeated experiments, she observed that the electrical effects of uranium rays were constant, and were unaffected either by light or heat, or by whether the uranium was solid or powdered, dry or wet, or pure or combined with other elements in a compound. By studying various compounds of uranium, she discovered that those with a higher proportion of uranium gave off the most intense radiation. In other words, the intensity of the rays depended only on the quantity of uranium in the compound, not on the physical or chemical properties of the compound itself.

A critical realization dawned on her. As she described it in a popular article that appeared in *Century Magazine* just over six years later, "I reached the conviction that the emission of rays by the compounds of uranium is a property of the metal itself—that it is an atomic property of the element uranium independent of its chemical or physical state." At the time, scientists still believed that atoms were indivisible, and they had no concept of the vast amounts of energy stored within atoms. Marie's idea was still in an embryonic form, but it was clear that something was going on within the uranium atom, and it was generating a form of energy that was different from the chemical energy scientists observed when different atoms combined.

Her next step was to see whether uranium was unique in its ability to ionize air or if other elements could also make air into a conductor of electricity. A number of chemists assisted her by putting at her disposal various specimens, some containing very rare elements. Her study of all the known elements revealed that not only uranium compounds but also thorium compounds emitted "Becquerel rays." With thorium as with uranium, the emission of rays seemed to be an atomic property. To describe the behavior of these two elements, Marie coined the word *radioactivity,* which first appeared in an article she published, along with Pierre and another colleague, in April 1898, less than four months after beginning her doctoral research.

Marie's study of mineral samples produced a further surprise, which she discussed in the same article: "Two minerals of uranium—pitchblende (uranium oxide) and chalcolite (copper uranyl phosphate)—are much more active than uranium itself. This fact is very remarkable and leads to the belief that these minerals may contain an element [that] is much more active than uranium."

Pierre was as intrigued by Marie's observation as she was. If a pitchblende sample was three or four times more radioactive than could be explained by the quantity of uranium it

text continues on page 41

When the French physicist Henri Becquerel (1852-1908) discovered "his" uranium rays in 1896 and when Marie Curie began to study them, one of the givens of physical science was that the atom was indivisible and unchangeable. The work of Becquerel and Curie soon led other scientists to suspect that this theory of the atom was untenable.

Scientists soon learned that some of the mysterious "rays" emanating from radioactive substances were not rays at all, but tiny particles. Radioactive atoms emit three different kinds of radiation. One kind of radiation, the alpha particle, has a positive electric charge and consists of two protons and two neutrons. It is thus the same as the nucleus of the helium atom, since helium nuclei contain two protons and two neutrons. Alpha particles exit radioactive nuclei with high energies, but their energy dissipates as they move through matter. An alpha particle can pass through a thin sheet of aluminum foil, but is stopped by anything thicker. Beta particles, a second form of radiation, are negatively charged electrons, which travel at nearly the speed of light. A beta particle can make its way through five centimeters of aluminum. Gamma rays, a third type of radiation, are true rays, or electromagnetic waves, as we would say today. They have no mass and no electrical charge and are similar to, but more energetic than, the X rays discovered by the German physicist Wilhelm Conrad Roentgen (1845–1923) in 1895. Gamma rays are also capable of deeper penetration of matter than alpha or beta particles. A gamma ray can pass through a meter of concrete or five centimeters of lead.

The point was that radioactivity was caused by the emission of tiny particles and energetic waves from the atomic nucleus. Building on Marie Curie's research, scientists soon realized that atoms are not indivisible and unchangeable, that atoms are made up of smaller particles, and that the nuclei of uranium and some other elements are unstable. Ernest Rutherford (1871–1937), working in Canada with his associate Frederick Soddy (1877–1956), began to develop a revolutionary hypothesis to explain the process of radioactive decay. Rutherford suggested that radioactive elements actually transform themselves into other elements. They spontaneously break apart, or decay, into the nuclei of other elements with smaller atomic masses. As they do so, they emit radiation from their nuclei in one or more of the three forms. The spontaneous decay process continues until a stable nucleus is formed.

In order to understand what happens when radioactive atoms emit radiation, it is important to understand what an isotope is. All atoms of the same element have the same number of protons in their nuclei, and thus the same atomic number. But atoms of the same element can have different numbers of neutrons, and thus different atomic masses. Isotopes of an element are forms of that element with different atomic masses. Hydrogen, for example, the lightest element, has the atomic number 1. It normally has one proton and no neutrons, and thus its atomic mass is also 1. But hydrogen has two isotopes with different atomic masses. Heavy hydrogen, or deuterium, has one proton and one neutron in its nucleus, and thus its atomic mass is 2. Hydrogen also has a radioactive isotope, tritium. Tritium has one proton and two neutrons, and thus its atomic mass is 3. Hydrogen and its isotopes have the same chemical properties. Similarly, all the isotopes of any element have the same chemical properties.

When a radioactive nucleus gives off alpha or beta particles, it changes into an atom of another element. For example, thorium (which Marie Curie identified as radioactive in April 1898) forms when uranium 238—an isotope of uranium with 92 protons and 146 neutrons—loses an alpha particle, which is the same as a helium nucleus. Since a helium nucleus consists of two protons and two neutrons, the result is a nucleus with 90 protons and 144 neutrons, or the isotope of thorium with an atomic mass of 234. The nucleus that undergoes decay is called the parent, and the nucleus into which it is transformed is called the daughter. In this transformation, the product of the radioactive decay of the parent uranium is the daughter thorium.

Ernest Rutherford worked to develop a hypothesis that would explain the process of radioactive decay.

RADIOACTIVITY: RADIATION, DECAY, ISOTOPES, AND USES

continued from previous page

Daughter nuclei may themselves be unstable, as is the case with thorium. The uranium decay process continues until the stable lead nucleus forms. Marie Curie's radium and polonium are also radioactive decay products, or daughters, of uranium.

Rutherford and Soddy figured out that every radioactive isotope has a specific half-life. In other words, half the nuclei in a given quantity of a radioactive isotope will decay in a specific period of time. The half-life of uranium 238 is 4.5 billion years, which means that over that immense period of time half the nuclei in a sample of uranium 238 will decay.

By contrast with the very long half-life of uranium 238, the half-life of the longest-lived polonium isotope, polonium 210, is only 138 days. This short half-life helps explain why Marie Curie was unable to isolate polonium. Even as she performed her meticulous fractional crystallizations, the polonium in her raw material was disappearing as a result of its rapid radioactive decay.

The early work of Pierre and Marie Curie led almost immediately to the use of radioactivity in medicine. Over the years, many other uses of radioactivity have been found. Scientists learned to use radioactive isotopes to bombard atoms and thus to uncover secrets of atomic structure. About 50 years ago, a scientist figured out that knowing the half-life of a radioactive isotope of carbon can reveal the ages of certain plant and animal remains. Since the amount of this radioactive isotope is replenished in a living thing as long as it is alive, analyzing how much of this isotope remained in dead plant and animal tissues revealed their ages. The method works for remains that are as much as 50,000 years old.

Radioactive isotopes are widely used not only in medicine and in scientific research but also in industry. Gamma rays, for example, can be used to reveal weak spots in oil-pipeline welds, and radiation from radioactive isotopes is used by the food industry to kill organisms that spoil food and cause disease.

text continued from page 37

contained, the pitchblende must contain an as-yet-undiscovered but highly radioactive element. His curiosity piqued, Pierre abandoned his work on crystals to help speed up the discovery of this new element. As Marie later noted in her autobiography, "Neither of us could foresee that in beginning this work we were to enter the path of a new science which we should follow for all our future." Nor could they anticipate just how difficult the task of finding the new substance would be. The difficulties arose in at least four areas: the complex chemical composition of pitchblende itself, the primitive laboratory facilities at their disposal, the expense of carrying out the research, and the decline in the Curies' health.

A Cornell University physicist, Professor Ernest Merritt, described the first problem in this way:

> The task undertaken by Mme. Curie in attempting to separate [the unknown substance] from pitchblende was somewhat similar to that of a detective who starts out to find a suspected criminal in a crowded street. Pitchblende is one of the most complex of minerals, containing twenty or thirty different elements, combined in a great variety of ways. The chemical properties of the suspected new element were entirely unknown; in fact, except for its one property of radioactivity, nothing whatever was known about it. The problem was one of extreme difficulty; but it had all the fascination of a journey into an unexplored land.

As Marie wrote in her biography of her husband, "Since the composition of this ore was known through very careful chemical analysis, we could expect to find, at a maximum, 1 percent of a new substance." But years of hard labor showed that their hopes for a yield as high as 1 percent were vastly exaggerated. "The result of our experiment proved that there were in reality new radioactive elements in pitchblende, but that their proportion did not reach even a millionth percent! . . . Would we have insisted, despite the scarcity of our means of research, if we had known the true proportion of what we were searching for, no one can tell; all that can be said now is that the constant progress of our work held us absorbed in a

These pages from Marie Curie's journal for June 1898, some two months after she coined the term radioactivity, contain measurements of the properties of various elements.

passionate research, while the difficulties were ever increasing."

In order to ferret out the hidden radioactive substances in pitchblende, Marie pioneered a technique of chemical analysis known as fractional crystallization. Boiling a strong solution of a substance and then cooling it causes the substance to form pure crystals when it solidifies again. For example, melting and then cooling a strong solution of sugar and water leads to the formation of pure sugar crystals, known as rock candy. Fractional crystallization takes advantage of the tendency of different substances in the same solution to form crystals at different temperatures, depending on their atomic weights, as the solution cools, with lighter elements crystallizing first.

As she made repeated fractional crystallizations of pitchblende, Marie used the Curie electrometer to test the various crystal solids for radioactivity, discarding those substances that were not active. In this way, she found that the greatest radioactivity was concentrated in two compounds, one containing bismuth and the other containing barium. The Curies concluded that each compound contained a hitherto unknown element. The first they named polonium, after Marie's native land, and they announced their discovery of polonium in July

1898. In December of that same year, they announced their discovery of the second new element, which they named radium. The Curies noted that the chemical properties of the two elements were entirely different from each other. What the new elements shared was a strong radioactivity.

The quest was not over, however. Marie believed that to prove the existence of the new elements to the satisfaction of the scientific world she would have to separate them from the bismuth and barium with which they were mixed. To do so, she would have to refine much larger quantities of pitchblende than they had.

The SIPC storeroom in which they had done their earlier investigations would no longer suffice. "Papa Schütz" had nothing better to offer them than an abandoned shed across the courtyard, which had once served as a dissecting room for the School of Medicine. There, under unbelievably difficult conditions, Marie succeeded in 1902 in preparing a tenth of a gram of pure radium chloride and in making a preliminary determination of the new element's atomic weight. (Her attempt to isolate polonium was not successful, for reasons that she did not yet understand.) She would later write that while it took her almost four years to establish the identity of radium as a new element, "One year would probably have been enough for the same purpose, if reasonable means had been at my disposal."

A visiting foreign scientist once described the Curies' SIPC laboratory as "a cross between a stable and a potato cellar and, if

The Curies conducted their groundbreaking research in this rude shed in the courtyard of the School of Industrial Physics and Chemistry in Paris (SIPC). Colleagues were often amazed at the primitive conditions in which Marie and Pierre labored.

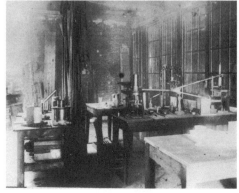

I had not seen the work table with the chemical apparatus, I would have thought it a practical joke." Nevertheless, in her biography of her husband and in her *Autobiographical Notes,* Marie described the shed that would be a second home to them for several years in terms that mingle frustration and longing:

> The only objects it contained were some worn pine tables, a cast-iron stove, which worked badly, and the blackboard which Pierre Curie loved to use. . . .
>
> Its glass roof did not afford complete shelter against rain; the heat was suffocating in summer, and the bitter cold of winter was only a little lessened by the iron stove, except in its immediate vicinity. There was no question of obtaining the needed proper apparatus in common use by chemists. . . .
>
> There were no hoods to carry away the poisonous gases thrown off in our chemical treatments, so that it was necessary to carry them on outside in the court, but when the weather was unfavorable we went on with them inside, leaving the windows open. . . .
>
> I had to work with as much as 20 kilograms of material at a time, so that the hangar was filled with great vessels full of precipitates and of liquids. It was exhausting work to move the containers about, to transfer the liquids, and to stir for hours at a time, with an iron bar, the boiling material in the cast-iron basin. . . .
>
> Yet it was in this miserable old shed that we passed the best and happiest years of our life, devoting our entire days to our work. Often I had to prepare our lunch in the shed, so as not to interrupt some particularly important operation. Sometimes I had to spend a whole day mixing a boiling mass with a heavy iron rod nearly as large as myself. I would be broken with fatigue at the day's end. Other days, on the contrary, the work would be a most minute and delicate fractional crystallization, in the effort to concentrate the radium. I was then annoyed by the floating dust of iron and coal from which I could not protect my precious products. But I shall never be able to express the joy of the untroubled quietness of this atmosphere of research and the excitement of actual progress with the confident hope of still better results.

As the radioactive substances from the fractional crystallization process became more and more concentrated, the Curies took special delight in returning to the shed at night. There the test tubes and capsules spontaneously glowed, emitting what Marie described as "faint, fairy lights." Eventually, Pierre noted that radium spontaneously emits not only light but also heat. As news of their work became known throughout the scientific world, particularly after their participation in a scientific conference in 1900, the possibility that atomic processes were generating the energy for such phenomena began to excite other scientists.

But no one, not even the most devoted scientists, can subsist on fairy lights alone, particularly with a young child and an elderly parent to provide for, a servant's salary to pay, and a major experiment to conduct without substantial outside support. Insufficient financial resources began to plague the Curies as never before. Pitchblende itself, the raw material for their research, was very expensive, and it was up to them to pay for it. Thanks to the intervention of the Academy of Sciences in Vienna, the Austrian government made a free gift to the Curies of a ton of pitchblende from which the uranium had already been removed, and agreed to make several more tons available at a good price. Of no interest to anyone until the Curies began to uncover the wondrous properties of radium, the pitchblende residues had been dumped into a pine forest near a mine at St. Joachimsthal in Bohemia. When the first shipment was delivered to the Curies' laboratory, Marie ripped open the bags and sifted through the pine needles, like an overeager child unwrapping birthday gifts. The Curies went on to process about seven tons of the pitchblende residues, learning the hard way that a ton contains only two to three tenths of a gram—or four to seven ten-thousandths of a pound—of radium.

Despite the help of the Austrian government and other subsequent support for their research, the Curies had realized shortly after Marie began her doctoral research that their

André Debierne in the Curies' laboratory shed at SIPC. He collaborated with them on their work on radioactivity. He remained Marie's devoted friend and colleague in the tumultuous years following Pierre's death and later helped direct research at the Radium Institute.

financial situation was shaky. Nonetheless, they agreed that it would be wrong to benefit personally from their scientific discoveries. Thus they did not patent any of their methods. They published unhesitatingly the details of all the processes they used to prepare radium. As scientists and then industrialists became interested in the Curies' work to advance their own goals, the couple continued to give out freely whatever information others requested. Within a short time a flourishing radium industry had developed, using the Curies' procedures, though the couple did not benefit financially from the boom they had initiated.

Instead, Pierre began to look for a better job. Since he was not a graduate of the "right" French schools, however, positions for which he was uniquely qualified were offered to others. In the spring of 1900, a tempting offer came from across the border, from the University of Geneva in Switzerland. It included a better than average salary for Pierre, the prospect of a well-equipped laboratory for their work, and an official position for Marie as well. Nonetheless, he turned down the offer, fearing that a move would interrupt their research. Anxious to prevent the Curies from abandoning France, the mathematician Henri Poincaré intervened, and Pierre was offered a position as chair of physics in the Sorbonne's required program for medical students. Because the program included physics, chemistry, and natural history, it was known colloquially as the PCN program. Pierre undertook the new position while continuing his work at SIPC. Marie wanted to do her part to supplement the family income, so she applied for and received the position of physics lecturer at a teachers' training institute for young women in the Paris suburb of Sèvres. She was the first woman to hold the position of lecturer there, and also the first to make experimental work part of the physics curriculum.

Although their income increased, the PCN position did not include a laboratory. Pierre found himself increasingly exhausted not only by his new course load but also by the daily trips between the shed at SIPC and his teaching quarters at PCN. In her biography of her husband, Marie recounted that "The physical fatigue due to the numerous courses he was obliged to give was so great that he suffered from attacks of acute pain, which in his overtaxed condition became more and more frequent." At this point, Marie did not entertain the possibility of a connection between Pierre's symptoms and the radioactive materials with which they were working. Today we know that even moderate doses of radiation can affect the body's immune system, and that the symptoms of radiation sickness can include general malaise, as well as much more serious disorders, including cancer. During the course of her thesis research, Marie lost nearly 20 pounds, and they both experienced permanent damage to their fingertips from handling the radium.

Marie's failure to face up to the possible link between radioactivity and the decline in their health is all the more puzzling because of her awareness of Pierre's trailblazing studies of the effects of radium on living organisms. After two German scientists announced that radioactive substances affected living tissue, Pierre intentionally burned his arm by exposing it to radium for several hours. The burn took several months to heal. Pierre concluded that exposure to radioactivity could kill diseased cells, and that radium could be used as a treatment for cancer and certain skin disorders. His studies led to the development of radiation therapy, which is in very widespread use today. But even as the Curies became famous for their discovery of the "miracle drug" radium, their unprotected bodies were being damaged by its radiation.

The decline in the Curies' health, however, did not dampen their excitement when, in March 1902, they made a triumphant discovery. By heating a test sample, they found that a certain color intensified that was not intensified in samples of other elements. They thus observed radium's spectrum, its personal "fingerprint." This important discovery proved that radium was indeed an element.

In addition to the decline in their physical health, other factors began to undermine the satisfaction they took in their work. Despite the acclaim their work was receiving elsewhere,

Marie Curie with some of her students at the teachers' training institute for women in Sèvres, where she was the first woman appointed to the faculty.

the French scientific establishment still seemed unwilling to recognize their contribution. Pierre, who hated having to blow his own horn, was persuaded in May 1902 to present himself as a candidate for membership in the prestigious French Academy of Sciences. Each candidate was expected to curry favor with the members of the Academy by making personal calls on each one individually. Although Pierre had been assured that his election was a foregone conclusion, a competitor was selected instead for the single vacancy. When one of Pierre's supporters later asked if he could nominate Pierre for the French Legion of Honor—France's highest order of merit to living people—Pierre declined. He had no need of a decoration, he told his friend, though he was sorely in need of a laboratory. Years later, after her own reputation had been secured both internationally and within France, Marie continued to feel bitter about France's treatment of her husband.

Strong feelings of personal loss also tainted Marie's sense of professional accomplishment. Shortly after she began her doctoral research, her sister Bronya had left France together with her husband to open a tuberculosis sanatorium in Austrian Poland. The pain of Bronya's departure was softened by the knowledge that they could still see each other, if only infrequently. Now, in May 1902, Marie saw her family bonds weaken in a more permanent way. While she was en route to Poland to see her father after he had had a difficult gallbladder operation, her beloved parent died. Arriving in Warsaw after his death, she demanded that the coffin be opened. She knelt over the corpse, accusing herself of selfishly abandoning him to pursue her career in France.

Despite these blows, Marie would look back on the period that was drawing to a close as the most satisfying time of her life. It was a time of youth, of struggle, and of discovery, and she would always remember that "miserable old shed" as the site of "such happy work days, despite their attendant difficulties."

This caricature of the Curies appeared in the December 22, 1904, edition of the magazine Vanity Fair. *By that time, their discovery of the so-called miracle cure of radium had made them famous.*

"A Growing Notoriety"

Marie Curie had what might be called a love-hate relationship with fame. She very much resented France's slowness to acknowledge Pierre Curie's scientific eminence. But the public's interest in their mutual work also distressed her. In her *Autobiographical Notes* she complained that "a growing notoriety, because of the announcement of our discoveries, began to trouble our quiet work in the laboratory, and, little by little, life became more difficult."

The "untroubled quietness" in which they worked had been breached as soon as word began to spread of the therapeutic potential of radium. A French industrialist decided to open a factory to produce radium for the medical profession. Marie wrote two decades later of the "entirely disinterested manner" in which the industrialist "placed at our disposition a little working place in his factory and a part of the means necessary for us to use it." She seems to have been unaware of how the industrialist took advantage of the Curies' expertise. She and Pierre did, of course, benefit from the industrialist's help, for Marie was now able to leave to factory personnel the backbreaking work of extracting the radium-rich barium from its mineral ores, and could concentrate on purification through fractional crystallization in the shed. But it was the industrial-ist, not the Curies, who made money through the sale of radi-um produced in the factory by workers trained by Marie "in the delicate processes of this manufacture."

Growing public awareness of what the press had started to call the Curies' "miracle cure" did not always please the two scientists. In 1902 they experienced their first skirmish with intrusive reporters, who violated the sanctity of their shed. The legend of Marie Curie began to take shape: the discovery of a promising cure for cancer had been brought about by the exhausting labor of a young, blond, foreign-born mother and wife, working for long hours under barely tolerable condi-tions, and for no wages. When news spread that the Curies were distraught at their inability to account for some missing radium, a cabaret act was born, featuring impersonators of Pierre and Marie searching on their hands and knees around their laboratory.

From the outset of Marie's thesis work, the Curies had been presenting the results of their research-in-progress to their scientific colleagues. The French Academy of Sciences had on three occasions recognized Marie's scientific promise by awarding her the prestigious Gegner prize, and the Institute of France had also paid tribute to her work with a significant cash award. Now both Curies suddenly found themselves win-ners of prestigious prizes from abroad as well. Invitations to lecture also began to arrive.

In June 1903 the Curies traveled to London as guests of the Royal Institution, which had invited Pierre to speak about radium at one of its "Friday Evening Discourses." Pierre's health had by this time deteriorated so severely that he had trouble dressing himself on the evening of his talk. Observers noted how ill he looked. Custom forbade a woman from addressing the audience, which included not only prominent scientists but also the cream of England's social elite. Pierre, however, carefully acknowledged his wife's major role in their joint work. The great British physicist Lord Kelvin, Pierre's longtime admirer, not only sat next to Marie at the lecture but also hosted a luncheon the following day in Pierre's honor. Husband and wife later entertained themselves by calculating how many state-of-the-art labs they could equip with the proceeds from selling the jewels worn by the members of British high society they met that weekend.

Later that month, Marie defended her thesis with distinction and became the first French woman to receive a doctorate. Her examining committee of two physicists and one chemist included two future Nobel prizewinners. Her sister Bronya, who made the trip from Poland to witness her sister's academic triumph, insisted that Marie buy a new dress for the

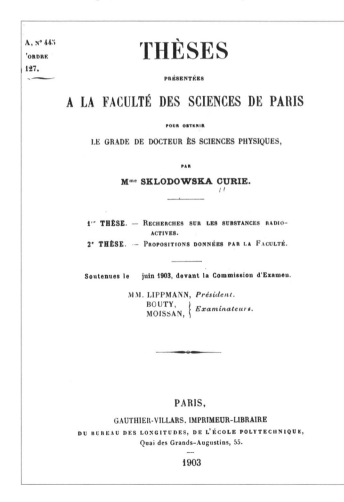

A, N° 445
'ORDRE
127.

THÈSES

PRÉSENTÉES

A LA FACULTÉ DES SCIENCES DE PARIS

POUR OBTENIR

LE GRADE DE DOCTEUR ÈS SCIENCES PHYSIQUES,

PAR

Mme SKLODOWSKA CURIE.

1'' THÈSE. — RECHERCHES SUR LES SUBSTANCES RADIO-ACTIVES.

2' THÈSE. — PROPOSITIONS DONNÉES PAR LA FACULTÉ.

Soutenues le   juin 1903, devant la Commission d'Examen.

MM. LIPPMANN, *Président.*
BOUTY, } *Examinateurs.*
MOISSAN, {

PARIS,

GAUTHIER-VILLARS. IMPRIMEUR-LIBRAIRE
DU BUREAU DES LONGITUDES, DE L'ÉCOLE POLYTECHNIQUE,
Quai des Grands-Augustins, 55.

1903

The title page of Marie Curie's doctoral thesis. The professors who evaluated her research—including one future Nobel Prize winner in physics and one in chemistry—said that Curie's work was the greatest contribution to science ever made by a doctoral thesis.

occasion. Marie chose a black one that—like her navy wedding outfit eight years earlier—could be serviceable in the laboratory afterward.

By this time, the Curies had become the focal point of a group of French scientists who met regularly at the Curies' home. The members of this group were invited to a celebratory dinner in Marie's honor held on the evening after her doctoral presentation at the home of Paul Langevin and his wife. Langevin, a former student of Pierre's, included on the guest list at the last minute a scientist of note from outside the Curie circle. Ernest Rutherford, the New Zealand–born British scientist whose nuclear theory of atomic structure was instrumental in shaping modern physics, happened to be in Paris with his wife. Rutherford dropped by the shed, only to learn that Marie was in the process of defending her thesis at the Sorbonne. During the dinner at the Langevins', Rutherford observed the radiation-damaged fingertips of both Curies. He asked Marie if it wasn't hard on them not having a real laboratory to work in. Rutherford could not have known that the search for a suitable laboratory would preoccupy Marie for years to come.

In November 1903 the Curies received two more awards from abroad. The Royal Society of London presented to the discoverers of polonium and radium its prestigious Davy Medal—named for the English chemist Humphrey Davy (1778–1829), who had himself discovered several chemical elements. The following month the Curies were awarded the Nobel Prize for physics for "their joint researches on the radiation phenomena discovered by Professor Henri Becquerel." Becquerel likewise shared in the prize, for "his discovery of spontaneous radioactivity."

Nobel Prizes were then, as now, made after debating the merits of the individuals whose names were put forward by a nominating committee. In the 1980s the Nobel archives made available for the first time the records of the 1903 debate. According to these records, the French Academy of Sciences was lobbying for a joint award to Becquerel and Pierre alone, omitting Marie. An influential Swedish physicist on the nominating committee alerted Pierre to the situation. If the prize had been for his research into magnetism, Pierre might not have objected. But as long as the award was to honor the research on radioactivity, he could not accept such an award without an acknowledgment of Marie's crucial role. He wrote back to his Swedish colleague, "If it is true that one is seriously thinking about me [for the prize], I very much wish to be considered with Madame Curie with respect to our research on radioactive bodies." Strictly speaking, Marie was not a legitimate candidate, since her name had not been put forward for the 1903 prize. Luckily, however, she had been twice nominated the year before, and one of those nominations was validated for current consideration.

The wording of the award was somewhat ingenious, for a special reason. The Royal Swedish Academy's intent was to award the Curies the physics prize for "their discovery of the spontaneously radioactive elements." Among the scientists on the nominating committee, however, the chemists insisted that "the discovery of such a singularly remarkable element as radium might eventually be considered for a Nobel Prize in chemistry." The 1903 prize for that reason did not refer to the Curies' discovery of polonium and radium. The way was thus left open for a possible second award in the future. (The Swedish scientist who won the 1903 Nobel Prize in chemistry himself considered the discovery of radium the single most significant occurrence in his field in the past century.)

The Curies were too ill to attend the December 1903 Nobel awards ceremony in Stockholm. Since recipients of the award are required to deliver a lecture discussing the significance of their work, the Curies finally made the trip in June 1905. Although, again, it was Pierre who delivered the lecture, he took pains to give credit to Marie for the work she did by herself, distinguishing subtly but carefully between her independent contributions and their joint discoveries.

KONGLIGA SVENSKA
VETENSKAPS-AKADEMIEN

ALFRED NOBEL

PIERRE CURIE
OCH HANS HUSTRU FRU
MARIE CURIE

Stockholm den 10 December 1903

In 1903, the Curies were awarded the Nobel Prize in physics for "their joint researches on the radiation phenomena discovered by Professor Henri Becquerel." Illness kept them from attending the December 1903 awards ceremony. Pierre finally made their acceptance speech in June 1905. He concluded with the hope "that mankind will derive more good than harm from the new discoveries."

Pierre's Nobel address was noteworthy for the cautionary comment with which he ended his speech. Perhaps radium's properties, if manipulated by the wrong hands, could unleash harm on the world, "and here the question can be raised whether mankind benefits from knowing the secrets of Nature, whether it is ready to profit from it, or whether this knowledge will not be harmful for it." Alluding to the invention of dynamite by Alfred B. Nobel, the Swedish industrialist whose fortune made the awards possible, Pierre pointed out that explosives are capable both of benefiting humanity and of leading to war. He concluded by saying, "I am one of those who believe with Nobel that mankind will derive more good than harm from the new discoveries."

In her biography of Pierre, Marie wrote of their mixed reaction to receiving the Nobel Prize. On the one hand, the award represented an "important" and even a "very happy" event for them—bringing with it not only prestige but also a considerable amount of money. (For the first time, they were able to hire and pay a lab assistant.) On the other hand, the prestige was a heavy burden. Journalists and photographers besieged them, not only at the laboratory but also at home. Just as in 1993 the American press considered the new American president's daughter, Chelsea Clinton, and even the family cat, Socks, to be fair game, so the French press of 1903 felt that it was only doing its job in quoting the Curies' daughter Irène, and photographing her and her cat, Didi, during her parents' absence from home. In her *Autobiographical Notes,* Marie acknowledged the good intentions of well-wishers whose visits, letters, and demands for information followed the award of the Nobel Prize. But she also complained that the "overturn of voluntary isolation was a cause of real suffering for us and had all the effect of disaster."

The notoriety was particularly troublesome for Pierre, whose health was a growing cause of concern. In a letter written in January 1904, a month after the award, Pierre wrote, "I long for calmer days passed in a quiet place, where lectures will be forbidden and newspapermen persecuted." In another letter, written a month after delivering his acceptance speech, he wrote, "A whole year has passed since I was able to do any work, and I have not one moment to myself. Evidently I have not yet found the way of defending us against frittering away our time, and yet it is very necessary. It is a question of life or death from the intellectual point of view." In fact, Pierre, who had published 25 papers between July 1898 and June 1904, published nothing in the following two years.

Despite the "serious trouble brought into the organization of our life" by "the invasion of publicity" following the Nobel Prize, the period between December 1903, when the award was announced, and June 1905, when Pierre gave his acceptance speech, included its share of satisfactions: a new professorship for Pierre and a new daughter for the Curie family.

Perhaps it was due only to embarrassment at France's failure to acknowledge Pierre's contributions in the face of such prestigious recognition from abroad, but whatever the reason, Pierre was finally made a professor at the Sorbonne, beginning with the academic year of 1904–05. Even this honor, however,

in its original terms, seemed a subtle blow to Pierre's dignity. The new chair in physics being created for Pierre did not come with laboratory facilities. Pierre wrote that he would therefore have to turn it down. His letter had the desired effect, and the Sorbonne found the funds not only for a lab but also for a staff of three assistants. The senior position of chief of laboratory was offered to Marie. For the first time, the Nobel prizewinner would be rewarded for her work not only with a title but also with a salary! Pleased though the Curies were by this turn of events, Marie noted in her biography of Pierre that it "was not without regret that we left the School of Physics," the site of their great work. In fact, since the decision to provide the Curies with a laboratory was an afterthought, Pierre assumed his new position before the new facility was constructed. He and Marie thus moved their apparatus from the old, familiar shed to another makeshift set of rooms.

In December 1904, a month after their move to the Sorbonne, the Curies' second daughter, Eve, was born. Marie had been deeply saddened following a miscarriage in August 1903. The birth of Eve, while it kept her from her research for a while, nonetheless brightened her outlook. Rather than being a burden, Eve's arrival seemed to infuse Marie with new energy. In comparing his physical stamina to Marie's, Pierre wrote to a friend in November 1905, "I get tired easily, and I no longer have more than a very feeble capacity for work. My wife, on the contrary, leads a most active life, between her children, the school at Sèvres and the laboratory. She does not lose a minute, and attends much more regularly than I do to the progress of the laboratory, in which she passes the greater part of her day." Marie also found energy to go to art exhibits and concerts. Pierre accompanied her without enthusiasm.

The Sorbonne appointment and the birth of Eve were followed in July 1905 by what should have been a third satisfaction: Pierre's election, on his second attempt, to the French Academy of Sciences. This honor, however, did little to lift Pierre's spirits or to increase his productivity. Expressing no pleasure at the Academy's belated recognition, Pierre instead wrote to a friend in October 1905, "I have not yet discovered what is the use of the Academy."

CHAPTER 5

"Honor Under Cruel Circumstances"

When Pierre left the house on Thursday, April 19, 1906, there was no way for Marie to know that she would never again see him alive. The family had just spent a delightful Easter holiday in the country, where Pierre had enjoyed the attempts of 8½-year-old Irène to catch butterflies in a little green net, and of 14-month-old Eve to remain surefooted on the bumpy terrain.

Despite his illness and depression of the past several years, Pierre was once again feeling involved in his work. Decades later, in her biography of her mother, Eve quoted a letter he wrote five days before his death, expressing guarded optimism that a new joint project with Marie was finally showing signs of success: "Madame Curie and I are working to dose [determine the exact quantity of] radium with precision by the amount of emanation [the name Rutherford had given to the radioactive gas emitted by a radioactive substance] it gives off. That might seem to be nothing, and yet here we have been at it for several months and are only now beginning to obtain regular results."

Pierre had several engagements to attend on his last day— a luncheon of the Association of Professors in the Faculty of

Science, a visit to his publisher to correct proofs, one appoint-ment in the afternoon, and another that evening with his physicist colleague and next-door neighbor Jean Perrin. He was fated to keep only the first engagement. Lunch with his fellow professors over, he went out into the rain and headed for his publisher, only to discover that the offices were shut because of a strike. As he walked on, fumbling with his umbrella, he slipped while crossing a busy street. The driver of a heavy horse-drawn cart pulled on his reins, but to no avail. The cart's rear wheel hit Pierre's head, crushing his skull. Death was instantaneous.

News of the fatal accident arrived shortly thereafter at the Curie home, but only Pierre's father was there to receive it. According to Eve, when he saw the faces of the bearers of bad news, her grandfather said, "My son is dead." After learning the cir-cumstances of Pierre's death, he added, "What was he dreaming of this time?"

Marie did not return home from the lab until six o'clock that evening, only to dis-cover the two visitors—Professor Perrin and the dean of faculty, Paul Appell—still sitting with her father-in-law. Paul Appell repeated the facts. After standing silently for what seemed an eternity, the 38-year-old widow said, "Pierre is dead? Dead? Absolutely dead?" Eve was later to analyze the transfor-mation that occurred in that moment: "Mme Curie, on that day in April, became not only a widow, but at the same time a pitiful and incurably lonely woman."

Marie nonetheless took charge. She asked Madame Perrin to take Irène next door for a few days, where she could be with the Perrin children. She sent a telegram to her family in Poland: "Pierre

In death, Pierre Curie was reunited with his beloved mother in the family plot in Sceaux, France. Although Marie Curie was buried in the same plot after her death in 1934, over 60 years later, in April 1995, she and Pierre were reburied in the Panthéon, the sepul-cher for eminent French persons, located in Paris.

dead result accident." She arranged to have Pierre's body brought back to the house. Only when Pierre's older brother, Jacques, arrived the next day from Montpellier did she allow herself to break down. The emotional outburst was brief.

Telegrams and letters began to arrive. Newspapers around the world carried the story. To enable those, like Lord Kelvin, her brother Joseph, and her sister Bronya, who set out hastily for Paris, to attend the funeral, she scheduled it for that Saturday, in the same cemetery where his mother lay. After the funeral and burial, she began a diary into which, for an entire year, she poured her emotions, addressing herself to her deceased husband in intimate terms. (The contents of the diary, which the family entrusted after Marie's death to the French National Library, were closed to researchers until 1990.)

The day after the funeral the French government officially offered to support Marie and the children with a state pension, as had been done for the widow of the great chemist and bacteriologist Louis Pasteur (1822–95). When Jacques informed her of the offer, she flatly rejected it, asserting her conviction that she could perfectly well support herself and her daughters.

Accompanied by Jacques, Marie returned to her research that very day. Eve later quoted Marie's diary entry describing that first attempt to resume productive work: "On the Sunday morning after your death, Pierre, I went to the laboratory with Jacques for the first time. I tried to make a measurement, for a graph on which we had each made several points. But I felt the impossibility of going on."

In her *Autobiographical Notes,* Marie summarized the emotional turmoil of those days: "It is impossible for me to express the profoundness and importance of the crisis brought into my life by the loss of the one who had been my closest companion and best friend. Crushed by the blow, I did not feel able to face the future. I could not forget, however, what my husband used to say, that, even deprived of him, I ought to continue my work."

Less than a month after Pierre's death, on May 13, 1906, the University of Paris, which had never before had a female professor, made an unprecedented offer to Marie. Pierre's academic position was hers, if she would have it. As she reported in her *Autobiographical Notes,* she hesitated before accepting. "The honor that now came to me was deeply painful under the cruel circumstances of its coming." Her sense that she could best pay homage to her deceased husband by resuming their research was instrumental in overcoming her hesitancy. In *Pierre Curie* she wrote, "I accepted this heavy heritage, in the hope that I might build up some day, in his memory, a laboratory worthy of him, which he had never had, but where others would be able to work to develop his idea."

Marie Curie with her daughters outside their new home in the village of Sceaux, where the family moved after Pierre's death.

The summer following Pierre's death was a busy one for Marie. She sent the girls off to the country with relatives and set about several tasks. She decided to move, together with her father-in-law, to Sceaux, where Pierre had lived with his parents when the couple first met, and where he and his mother were now buried. The move would mean a half-hour commute to work, but she felt it would be better for the family to be in new surroundings. She also faced two formidable professional challenges: to prepare a course justifying her professorial position and to refute a devastating criticism of her work from an unexpected quarter—Pierre's longtime supporter, Lord Kelvin.

The first challenge was the less daunting of the two. In the course of the summer, Marie went over Pierre's teaching notes, as well as other professional materials. An hour and a half before her first lecture at the Sorbonne, on November 5, 1906—15 years to the day after she had first enrolled there as a student—Marie stood in the cemetery at Sceaux by Pierre's tomb. Meanwhile, crowds began to fill the lecture hall, not only students but also many curious onlookers who, having been alerted by the press, were eager to hear what the Sorbonne's first woman professor would say, and how the mourning wife would acquit herself. Those expecting high drama were doubtless disappointed when the small woman entered the room and, waiting for the spontaneous applause to die down, began to speak. Picking up Pierre's course exactly where he had left it, she began, "When one considers the progress that has been made in physics in the past ten years, one is surprised at the advance that has taken place in our ideas concerning electricity and matter. . . ."

The second challenge was issued in an unconventional manner. Lord Kelvin had decided that radium was not an element at all, but more likely a compound of lead and five helium atoms. Because of the popular interest in radium, he published his theory not in a scientific journal but in the "Letters to the Editor" column on the front page of the

London Times. Lord Kelvin's theory threatened to undermine not only Marie's entire scientific career but also Rutherford's work in explaining the phenomenon of radioactivity. Marie responded not in words but by setting out to prove in the laboratory that radium indeed merited its own spot in the periodic table. With the help of André Debierne, who had been a colleague of the Curies from the earliest days in the SIPC storeroom, she succeeded in 1910 in isolating pure radium metal. To do so meant separating radium from its salts, even though radium was only stable as long as it was chemically combined in a salt. The difficult process, which risked the loss of precious radium, was never again repeated, but it proved its point. Lord Kelvin, having died in 1907, spared himself the embarrassment of being proved wrong.

While the determination to vindicate her claims about radium propelled her forward in the months after Pierre's death, other professional satisfactions came her way. Two in particular advanced her goal of building a laboratory worthy of Pierre. In the winter of 1907, some months after meeting Marie Curie in Paris, the American philanthropist Andrew Carnegie sent Dean Paul Appell $50,000 to found the Curie Scholarships. These fellowships, which would enable promising scientists to devote themselves full-time to research, helped Marie put together a research staff. In choosing the Curie scholars, she always had an eye out for talented Poles and talented women. Then, in 1909, the Pasteur Institute—interested in radium's medical applications—and the University of Paris began discussions about founding a Radium Institute. Within a few years the arrangements were made. The two institutions would share equally in the cost of establishing the Institute, which would consist of two divisions—a radioactivity laboratory under Marie's supervision, and a medical research laboratory under the supervision of an eminent physician.

Her intensive laboratory work and teaching preparations made it necessary for Marie to give up her teaching at the school in Sèvres for women teachers-in-training, where her

Irène Curie points to visible evidence of her mother's devotion to her work: her radiation-scarred fingertips.

friend and colleague Paul Langevin replaced her. But Marie in these years undertook another course of teaching closer to home. Dissatisfied with the methods of the schools she looked at for Irène, she decided with a group of like-minded professional parents to run a cooperative school, with the parents teaching the children in their fields of specialization. For two years, Irène, along with eight or nine other children, thus studied mathematics, chemistry, physics, French history and literature, art history, and studio art, taught by some of the great practitioners of the time.

The death of Pierre's father in February 1910 dealt a severe blow to Marie. Dr. Curie had been instrumental not only in caring for both girls but also in imbuing Irène, the older of the two, with his values. For the next several years, Marie would share the responsibilities of the girls' upbringing with a succession of Polish governesses, some more successful than others.

But that year of intense mourning also was a year of achievement. In addition to her triumph in isolating pure radium metal, Marie was awarded five honorary titles, as well as a medal from the Royal Society of Arts in London. That fall, at an international professional meeting in Belgium, Marie was given the prestigious responsibility of defining the international standard for measuring radium. Such a standard was needed in order to ensure the success of radium therapy, as well as for industrial purposes and scientific research. Although not everyone agreed, Marie insisted that since it had already been determined that the standard unit was to be called a "curie," she and she alone should define it. Using a carefully weighed amount of pure radium salt, she prepared the standard curie the following year. Although originally defined as the amount of radiation emitted by 1 gram of radium, a curie is now defined as 37 billion atomic decays per second. Shortly after returning to Paris, Marie also took pleasure in the publication of her monumental *Treatise on Radioactivity.* Rutherford reviewed the two-volume work favorably, although privately he questioned its long-term utility, since it was heavy on specific details and short on critical analysis.

Marie Curie was able to go on living after the devastating blow dealt her in April 1906 because of her work. In *Pierre Curie,* Marie described conversations she and Pierre sometimes had in the early days of their marriage, when one or the other entertained thoughts of irreparable loss. According to Marie, Pierre always offered the same response: "Whatever happens, even if one should become like a body without a soul, still one must always work." By taking Pierre's advice to heart, Marie was able to continue functioning—if never to give up grieving—after his untimely death.

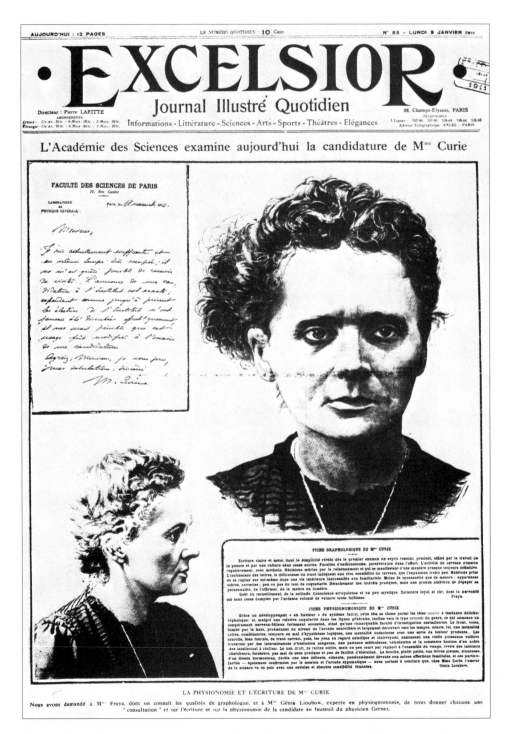

Attacks on Marie Curie's ancestry and character, such as this one on the front page of the January 9, 1911, edition of the daily newspaper Excelsior, cost her a place in the French Academy of Sciences.

"Grave Illness"

By the end of 1910, Marie Curie seemed to be well on her way to recovery from her shocking loss. She had established herself as a university professor. Her dream of establishing a Radium Institute in Pierre's honor was beginning to be realized. No one could have anticipated that the year that followed would bring with it emotional setbacks of such severity that even an unprecedented second Nobel Prize could not prevent a downward spiral into mental and physical decline.

At the core of Marie Curie's problem was the attitude of the press that such a well-known personage was legitimate prey. Just as journalists today seek to uncover every wart on every public figure, the French newspapers of the time were often overeager in their attempt to woo readers with fresh news of scandal. And Marie Curie made for very good press indeed for well over a year, beginning with the announcement in November 1910 of her candidacy for the single vacant seat for a physicist in the French Academy of Sciences.

Another candidate for the empty seat was Edouard Branly (1844–1940), a 66-year-old physicist who in 1904 had shared in a prestigious French award with Marie. (Ironically enough, the award was given by the Paris Press Syndicate.) In 1890 Branly had pioneered a device that Guglielmo Marconi (1874–1937) later incorporated into his "wireless telegraph," the first radio. When Marconi received the Nobel Prize for physics in 1909, many French citizens felt that their national pride had been wounded by Branly's exclusion from the prize. Many French citizens also admired Branly as much for his religious fervor as for his scientific contributions. Branly, a devout Catholic, was not only a professor at the Catholic Institute but also Commander of the Order of Saint Gregory the Great, an honor conferred on him by none other than the pope.

Like Pierre before her, Marie found distasteful the custom requiring candidates to the Academy to pay personal visits to each sitting member. Nonetheless, she swallowed her pride and began the humiliating chore, visiting even the man whom Pierre Curie had defeated in the 1905 election, who was one of Branly's chief supporters. Then, on January 10, 1911, 13 days before the Academy was to select its candidate, a nationalistic and anti-Semitic newspaper published its first attack on Marie, and other right-wing newspapers jumped on the bandwagon. The attack went beyond Marie's foreign origins to suggest that she was really Jewish—in either case, that she was not truly French, and thus was unworthy of membership in the French Academy. Some papers claimed that it was Pierre who had done all the work and that she had won the Nobel Prize only by clinging to his coattails. The liberal press came to Marie's defense, but the attacks stung nonetheless.

The election on January 23 was a major media event, with journalists, photographers, and curious spectators thronging the hall outside the room where the ballots were cast. In the final tally, Marie lost to Branly by two votes. The Academy was not to admit its first woman until 1979.

So confident had Marie's supporters been of her election that her staff had purchased a floral bouquet in advance. When Marie received the news of her defeat over the laboratory telephone, no one said a word, but the flowers were discreetly shoved under a workbench. Not only did Marie refuse to publish in the journal of the Academy for the next decade, but she never again renewed her candidacy. In her *Autobiographical Notes,* she—who had been admitted to membership in so many other distinguished societies without any need to grovel—spoke of her "strong distaste for the personal solicitation required" by Academy custom. She expressed her preference for academies that choose their members "based wholly on a spontaneous decision, without any personal efforts involved." (In fact, on February 7, 1922, the Academy of Medicine of Paris overturned precedent and elected her spontaneously to its vacant chair, "in recognition for the part she played in discovering radium and a new form of medical treatment.")

As one might expect, Marie put the distressing incident behind her by throwing herself into her work. Among other projects, she was working on a series of experiments in collaboration with her older Dutch colleague Heike Kamerlingh Onnes (1853–1926). Together with Kamerlingh Onnes, who was to win the Nobel Prize in 1913 for his work on low-temperature physics and his production of liquid helium, Marie hoped to study radiation from radium at low temperatures. But for more than a year, as revealed in her lab notebook, where there are no entries at all between October 7, 1911, and December 3, 1912, Marie experienced an uncharacteristic inability to work.

This silence was a result of the reaction of the press to the sole romantic relationship Marie ever allowed herself after Pierre's death. Paul Langevin, one of Pierre's former pupils, had been a close colleague and friend of the Curies for many years. Although his career was progressing with remarkable success, the same could not be said of his marriage. Both Paul and Jeanne Langevin were from working-class backgrounds, but while Paul's scientific gifts had won him prestigious scholarships, Jeanne lagged behind him in education. The Langevins had four children to support, and Madame Langevin accused her husband of negligence for choosing to stay in academic research, with its relatively low salaries, when he had been offered several high-paying jobs in industry. So strained did the relationship between husband and wife become that Langevin eventually moved out of the suburban

Paul Langevin, a former student of Pierre Curie's became a colleague and close friend of both Pierre and Marie. After Pierre's death, the friendship between Langevin and Marie eventually turned to love.

family house and took a small apartment in Paris, about half a mile from Marie's laboratory. Marie often left the laboratory at noon, picked up a few groceries, and proceeded to Langevin's apartment—which they called "our place"—to prepare lunch for the two of them.

Evidence suggests that Marie cared for Langevin deeply and that he reciprocated her profound affection. This woman, who had almost always worn dark colors even before becoming a widow, showed up one evening at a party of friends wearing a white dress with a rose at her waist, and a bloom on her cheek as well. She spoke confidentially to a woman friend about Jeanne Langevin's inability to understand her husband's commitment to research. She and Langevin exchanged letters, which one of his sons later burned. Some of those letters, however, or forgeries based on them, were stolen from Langevin's apartment and leaked to the press.

Rumors about the relationship began to spread during the summer of 1911, and soon Madame Langevin began legal proceedings to secure a separation from her husband. In late October, Marie Curie and Langevin, along with about 30 other top physicists from other countries, traveled to Brussels for the first of many physics conferences organized and paid for by the Belgian industrialist and philanthropist Ernest Solvay. The theme of the conference was the challenge facing physics as a result of the discovery of radioactivity and other phenomena that implied new mysteries about the atom. The participants heard Albert Einstein deliver a paper, which left Marie with a very high regard for the young scientist. Einstein had already published a paper in 1905 on his theory of special relativity, and at this point in his career he was a brilliant young scientist still looking for an appropriate academic position. Despite her personal problems in the weeks following the meeting, Marie made time on November 17 to write a letter of recommendation on Einstein's behalf for a position at the University of Zurich. Also at the First Solvay Congress, Marie allowed Ernest Rutherford to convince her to have the international radium standard she was working on stored not in her laboratory but at the Office of Weights and Measures at Sèvres.

On November 4, while the meeting was going on in Brussels, the Paris press broke the story of the Langevin-Curie liaison. In the days that followed, Paris awoke to headlines like "A Novel in a Laboratory: The Love Affair of Mme Curie and M. Langevin." Marie was derided as "The Vestal Virgin of Radium." Once again her foreign origins, and false suggestions that she was of Jewish ancestry, were held against her, with some reporters claiming that the home of a good Frenchwoman had been wrecked by a Jewish foreigner. Some newspapers even suggested that the affair had predated Pierre's

In November 1911, Curie (seated next to mathematician Henri Poincaré) and Langevin (standing at far right) attended the first Solvay conference, where they were greatly impressed by a talk delivered by the brilliant young physicist Albert Einstein (standing, second from right, next to Langevin).

death, and that the words of the driver under the wheels of whose cart Pierre had died—"He literally threw himself under my horse!"—proved that Pierre had committed suicide in despair. Several papers suggested that Marie's behavior had tarnished the Curie family name, an accusation that she took to heart.

French reporters tracked down the supposed lovers in Brussels. Despite their indignant response, and the support shown by many of their colleagues, Marie was upset enough to slip away from the conference before the closing session. Evading the reporters' watchful eyes, she made it back home. What she found there was terrifying. Incited by what they had been reading in the press, angry French citizens stood outside her home at Sceaux, traumatizing 14-year-old Irène and 7-year-old Eve. Some threw stones at the house. Others chanted, "Get the foreign woman out."

Marie packed up the girls and went to Paris, to the home of her friends the Borels. Emile Borel, a mathematician, was

scientific director of France's most prestigious college, and lived in an apartment provided by the Ministry of Public Instruction. His young wife, Marguerite, was the daughter of Paul Appell, the dean of the Sorbonne science faculty (and one of those to break the news of Pierre's death to Marie). The minister of public instruction threatened to fire Borel for sheltering the disreputable Madame Curie in an official apartment and thus sullying French academic honor. But the Borels refused to turn Marie out. Marguerite even threatened never to see her father again if he followed through on his plan to advise Marie to resign her professorship and return to Poland.

As if the matter were not complicated enough, several duels were fought over what Marie would later refer to, in her single written reference to it, as the "L. affair." As if in a farce, distinguished scientists challenged mediocre journalists, and journalists on the right challenged journalists on the left. A few participants were wounded, but no one was killed.

On November 7, shortly after the press seized on the story, Marie received a telegram bringing what in more tranquil times would have been wonderful news. The Nobel Prize for chemistry had been awarded to her "in recognition of her services in the advancement of chemistry by the discovery of the elements radium and polonium, by the isolation of radium and the study of the nature and compounds of this remarkable element." Whether or not Marie Curie truly deserved this second award has been the subject of much debate, since the work was essentially the same for which the earlier physics prize had been awarded. Furthermore, her work since the

1903 award had been solid but not groundbreaking. It is likely that an influential Swedish physicist on the Nobel committee had heard about the scandal and its effect on Marie, and had decided to show the world the esteem in which the scientific community still held the beleaguered woman. Ironically, as the scandal deepened, this same supporter began to sing a different tune. In a letter, he advised Marie that she should decline the prize until it had been proven that the accusations made about her relationship with Langevin were false. In a dignified response she indicated why she would not accept his advice: it was her science, not her personal conduct, that had been deemed worthy of honor. The value of her discovery should in no way be diminished by rumors about her private life. Therefore, she *would* accept the prize.

More welcome at the moment than the news of her second Nobel Prize, however, was the personal support she received from her closest friends and relatives. Pierre's brother, Jacques, once again made the trip from Montpellier to be by her side. Not only the Borels, but also her old friends the Perrins, and her trusted colleague André Debierne, did their best to calm the troubled academic waters. Little by little the public lost interest. Despite the arguments of her siblings, all of whom had traveled to Paris to persuade her to leave France for a position at Warsaw University, Marie decided to remain in France. To flee, she feared, might have been perceived as an admission that she had indeed wrecked the Langevin marriage. She would leave the country, she told them, but only to go to Stockholm to receive her award. As traveling companions, she took her daughter Irène and her sister Bronya.

At the award ceremony on December 10, the president of the Royal Swedish Academy of Sciences explained the Academy's decision to offer a Nobel laureate a second prize for essentially the same work. He noted that the discovery of radium had revolutionized scientists' understanding of the nature of matter. It had overturned the long-held belief that atoms are unchanging by showing that one element can transform itself into another. Pointing to the way in which the study of radium had opened up new areas of medicine, he concluded that Marie Curie's work deserved this additional recognition.

In her lecture the next day, Marie was careful to distinguish between her personal contributions to the prizewinning work and those of Pierre. But now sensitive to accusations that she had dragged Pierre's name through the mud, she took pains to state her assumption "that the award of this high distinction to me is motivated by [our] common work and thus pays homage to the memory of Pierre Curie." She also acknowledged the contributions of others, notably Rutherford, in explaining the phenomenon of radioactivity, but reasserted her claim to have been the first to see that it was an atomic property. She concluded her address by noting the changes in chemistry since the discovery of radioactivity. Once researchers worked with materials they could observe and measure; now a new era of "the chemistry of the imponderable" had dawned.

This photograph of Curie was taken in 1912, not long after she received a second Nobel Prize, this time in chemistry.

Upon her return to France, Marie fell desperately ill. In her *Autobiographical Notes,* at a distance of over 20 years, she omitted all mention of Langevin and merely wrote: "As a result of all the cares devolving on me, I fell seriously ill at the end of 1911. . . . Suffering though I was, I went to Stockholm to receive the prize. The journey was extremely painful for me. . . . A most generous reception was accorded me . . . but I was suffering so much that when I returned I had to stay in bed for several months."

She was suffering not only from deep depression but also from acute kidney problems, which may have been a symptom of radiation sickness. On December 29, 1911, she was taken on a stretcher to a private clinic, where she registered under an assumed name. Although by the end of January 1912 she had returned to her children, who had been forbidden to visit her in the clinic, she was too ill the following month to attend a physics conference in Paris. Debierne spoke there on her behalf about details of the international radium standard. In March she was back in the hospital for a kidney operation, which sapped both her physical and mental strength. During the months of recuperation in a rented house near Paris, she used the name Madame Sklodowska, feeling unworthy of the name Curie, forbidding even Irène to write to her using her married name. A relapse toward the end of June meant a move to a sanatorium, where she stayed for over a month.

By August, Marie felt physically and emotionally strong enough to accept an invitation to go to England and stay with a friend who had much in common with her. Hertha Ayrton was not only a physicist but also the widow of a physicist. Still using the name Sklodowska, Marie was able to spend over two months with Hertha without having the press pick up her scent. She felt sufficiently heartened by her recovery to welcome a visit from her daughters. (When, a year later, Marie paid another visit to England, to receive an honorary doctorate from the University of Birmingham and to meet again with Rutherford, she traveled as Madame Curie, much to Irène's relief.)

In October 1912, Marie returned to France, not to the house in Sceaux, but to an apartment in Paris, where she would spend her remaining years. She returned to her laboratory in early December and resumed her teaching at the Sorbonne after the holidays. The university administration, which had breathed a sigh of relief when Madame Langevin failed to mention Madame Curie by name in the separation agreement, was now willing to welcome the world's only double Nobel laureate into its groves.

Whatever relationship Paul Langevin and Marie Curie once had, neither he nor any other man was ever to have anything but merely friendly or strictly professional ties with her from now on. When World War I broke out in 1914, Langevin returned to his family. However, one can infer that his relationship with his wife had not really improved from a situation that occurred some years later, when Langevin had a child with one of his former students.

He asked Marie to find a position in her laboratory for his lover, and Marie complied. Interestingly enough, Marie's granddaughter Hélène later married Michel Langevin, Paul's grandson.

What Marie called her "grave illness" was now over. She turned her attention to the construction of the Radium Institute, to be jointly run by the Pasteur Institute and the University of Paris. Most of the rest of her life was devoted to shaping into a productive team as many promising scientists as she could afford to finance, in the institute she envisioned as a tribute "to the memory of Pierre Curie and to the highest interest of humanity."

Recovered from a long bout with illness and emotional distress, Curie (seated, center) traveled to Birmingham, England, in September 1913 to receive an honorary degree.

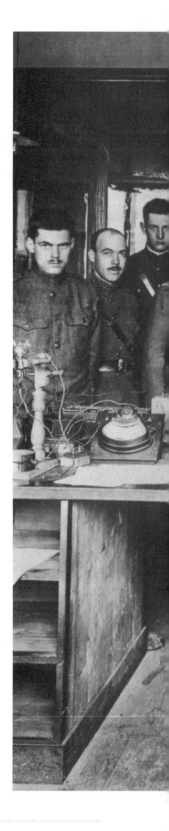

"The Hospital Life of Those Years"

By the end of August 1914, construction of the Radium Institute, on the newly named rue Pierre Curie, was completed. But earlier that month, on August 4, World War I had begun. All able-bodied men, including Madame Curie's entire laboratory staff, had been mobilized for war. Only an elderly mechanic with serious cardiac problems remained.

On September 2, three German bombs fell on Paris. A German plane also dropped a banner calling on Parisians to surrender. The president of France decided to move the government from Paris to Bordeaux, and many Parisians fled the capital along with the government. Marie had no intention of following that course, but she was concerned for the safety of the only supply of radium in France—the single gram that she had in her laboratory. At the government's request, she packed it up in a 45-pound lead box and boarded a train filled with fleeing government employees. As she looked out the train window, she saw the long line of automobiles waiting to leave the city. Having succeeded in entrusting the precious element to a Bordeaux bank safe-deposit box, she managed to get passage back to Paris on a military train. She noted in her *Autobiographical Notes* that French citizens at the Bordeaux train

Curie meets with a contingent of U.S. officers in her laboratory. During World War I, Curie enlisted her scientific knowledge in the service of the Allied war effort. With Irène's assistance she trained these Americans to use X rays and radiological equipment.

station "seemed surprised and comforted to learn of someone who found it natural to return to Paris."

Marie felt that she had important work to do there, even though to carry it out meant a separation from her children, who were spending the summer with their Polish cook and housekeeper in Brittany. Whatever resentments Marie might have felt toward France for its neglect of Pierre's gifts or for its treatment of her during the Langevin affair, she put them aside. As she wrote in her *Autobiographical Notes*, "The dominant duty imposed on every one at that time was to help the country in whatever way possible during the extreme crisis that it faced. . . . It was left to each to take his own initiative and means of action. I therefore sought to discover the most efficient way to do useful work."

Her first undertaking was to put X-ray technology to use in military hospitals. Although she had never worked with X rays herself, she had given several lectures on them each year in her course at the Sorbonne. Anticipating that the war would be a long one and that there would be many casualties, she foresaw how X rays could save lives by helping doctors locate bullets, shrapnel, and broken bones. Aware of the fact that there were only a few radiology centers for the medical use of X rays in civilian hospitals and none at all in the military, she persuaded the government to empower her to requisition equipment and to give her an official title—Director of the Red Cross Radiology Service—that would open doors for her.

During August and September 1914, Marie thus set about putting together the needed apparatus by hook or by crook. She had also realized that stationary radiology installations in hospitals would have to be supplemented by mobile ones that could bring X-ray apparatus to the wounded at the battlefront. To achieve her aims, she shamelessly approached wealthy acquaintances and asked not only for their money but also for their cars. She implored body shops to transform those cars into ambulance-like vans. She commandeered useful machinery from empty labs at the Sorbonne and also appealed to the patriotic instincts of manufacturers of scientific equipment. In this way, she secured what she needed for her radiology vehicles—soon to be called *petites Curie* by the French enlisted men.

In whatever spare time she had, she filled in gaps in various areas of her own knowledge. To make sure that she would be a qualified radiologist, she studied not only technical books on the use of X-ray apparatus but also anatomy textbooks. She also learned how to drive a car, earned her driver's license, and studied auto mechanics so that she would not have to rely on others in case she experienced car problems. Judging that 17-year-old Irène, who had been begging her mother for permission to join her in Paris, might be useful in the effort, Marie allowed her daughter to make the trip herself.

Marie's first *petite Curie* was roadworthy and fully equipped, complete with a red cross on its side, by late October 1914. Eventually, Marie was responsible for equipping 20 such vehicles (including one briefly in the charge of her friend and colleague Jean Perrin) and for establishing 200 stationary X-ray stations. Literally millions of wounded soldiers were examined in these facilities.

Marie's first radiological assistant was Irène, and their experiences at the front brought them closer together than

Through her unflagging wartime efforts, Curie was able to equip 20 motor vehicles as portable X-ray stations for use at the front. These vehicles became known as petites Curie.

ever before. In her *Autobiographical Notes,* Marie noted, "Of the hospital life of those years, we keep many a remembrance, my daughter and I." In October–November 1914 mother and daughter went to the battlefront in their *petite Curie,* accompanied by a military doctor. The car was fitted with an electric generator, a portable X-ray machine, photographic equipment, and a cable. The van's driver operated the generator, which remained in the vehicle. The cable connected the generator to the X-ray machine, which was set up in a room whose windows were darkened by curtains. Marie and Irène helped position the wounded in front of the equipment. Completely absorbed in their task, neither woman was fully aware of the dangers of overexposure to X rays. Although they wore cloth gloves, set up a few small metal screens, and avoided the direct beam when they could, they were inadequately shielded.

Sensing how upset Irène might be by seeing the terrible wounds of the soldiers, some of whom were no older than she, Marie was a model of detachment. Without emotion, she kept careful records of the data relating to each patient. Irène followed suit. A year later, Marie was confident enough in Irène's skill to leave her in charge of an X-ray installation on a second battlefront. After this, Irène did other solo stints, which often pitted the teenager against much older surgeons who were suspicious of the newfangled technology. By 1916, however, Marie had thought of a more important way for Irène to assist.

Marie had by then realized that radiological installations were useless without trained personnel to run them, and she decided to instruct women in the necessary techniques on the premises of the Radium Institute. In groups of about 20, the women took six-week courses that exposed them to the required basics of mathematics, physics, and anatomy. Irène, enrolled in her own course of study at the Sorbonne, helped her mother teach these courses, which produced 150 radiological technicians.

Meanwhile, Marie had come up with a plan to use her intimate knowledge of radium for the war effort. When the

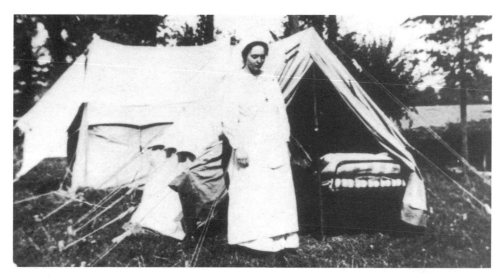

Irène Curie worked with her mother as a radiological assistant at the front during World War I.

threat of a German invasion of Paris did not materialize, Marie retrieved the gram of radium from Bordeaux and brought it back to the Radium Institute. There she began to use a technique developed by a scientist in Dublin to collect radon, a radioactive gas that is spontaneously emitted by radium. Although radon's therapeutic benefits had already been shown to be similar to those of radium, in some ways, as Marie noted in her *Autobiographical Notes,* radium therapy utilizing radon is "more practicable than the direct use of radium."

Radium emits radon steadily, and so every 48 hours Marie, working alone, used an electric pump to draw off the gas, sealing it in thin glass tubes about one centimeter long. Doctors at army and civilian hospitals used these tubes to help scar tissue form over certain types of wounds by encasing a tube in a platinum needle and positioning it inside a patient's body in the precise location where the radiation would be most effective.

Marie's description of the delicate procedure for preparing the tubes is noteworthy for being one of the rare references she made to the health hazards of radiation. In her *Autobiographical Notes* she wrote, "Since the handling of radium is far from being free of danger (several times I have felt a dis-

text continues on page 88

Radon is a gaseous element that does not combine easily with other chemicals. Although it has 28 known isotopes, only three of these occur in nature. The remaining 25 are produced artificially in nuclear reactors. (The ability of scientists to produce artificial radioactive isotopes developed as a result of work done in 1934 by Marie Curie's daughter, Irène, and her husband, Frédéric Joliot-Curie, who added his wife's last name to his own.)

The three naturally occurring isotopes of radon were discovered within a few years of Marie Curie's discovery of radium. In 1899 Ernest Rutherford and a colleague discovered a radon isotope while studying the radioactivity of thorium compounds. The half-life of this isotope is just under one minute. The following year, German chemist Friedrich E. Dorn discovered the radon isotope with the longest half-life, nearly four days. In 1904 Marie Curie's colleague André Debierne detected a third radon isotope in connection with his work on actinium, a radioactive element that he had discovered in 1899 in the leftover pitchblende from which the Curies had removed the radium. Debierne's isotope has the shortest half-life of any of the natural radon isotopes: under four seconds. Sometimes the name thoron is used for Rutherford's radon isotope, and actinon for Debierne's, with the name radon reserved for Dorn's isotope. All three natural isotopes of radon have very short half-lives.

By the time Pierre Curie gave his Nobel lecture in 1905, he was able to report that Rutherford had given the name "emanation" to the radioactive gas given off by a radioactive substance, and that these emanations decayed in a similar manner to their radioactive sources. In 1914 the Irish geologist and physicist John Joly (1857–1933) developed a method for "milking" the radon from radium by pumping it off, purifying it, compressing it, and encasing it in a glass tube. Joly also was first to see radon's potential for treating cancer victims. The glass tube encasing the radon emits penetrating gamma rays, which come primarily from bismuth 214, one of the decay products of radon.

Since the late 1980s, scientists have been more concerned with the health hazard associated with radon than with its therapeutic benefits. Radon is now considered to be the most prevalent cause of lung cancer in the United States among nonsmokers. The United States Environmental Protection Agency found that radon can be a source of indoor air pollution in buildings constructed above rocks and soil with high deposits of uranium, radium's parent. Radon can seep through cracks in foundation walls and floors. The radon can accumulate, exposing the people inside to radiation as it decays. The energy-efficient homes that have become more popular in recent years tend to accumulate radon more than other homes because they are less well ventilated.

Radioactivity from radon in houses is usually measured in picocuries, with "pico" meaning one-trillionth. Homeowners often have their homes tested for the level of radon accumulation. If radon is present in very high concentrations, more than four picocuries, a homeowner can seal cracks, install a gas vent below the foundation, and improve ventilation by bringing in outdoor air at a greater rate. Special vents can exchange outside air for the radon-laden inside air without jettisoning all the energy already used to heat the house.

The brief message on
this postcard was
Curie's 1915 assurance
to her younger daugh-
ter, Eve, that she was
safe and well despite
her dangerous work at
the front.

text continued from page 85

comfort which I consider a result of this cause), measures were taken to prevent harmful effects of the rays on the persons preparing emanations." At the same time, however, Marie attributed the exhaustion she felt after each radon-collecting session to the simple physical difficulty of the task. More likely, it was a result of her failure to protect herself adequately from the radon in the air she was inhaling.

Marie was eager to help the war effort as an ordinary citizen as well as a scientist. When the government asked people to contribute their gold and silver, Marie—lacking a wedding band—decided to offer all the medals she had received over the years, including her two Nobels. Although the French National Bank refused to accept the medals, Marie was able to contribute to the war effort by taking most of the prize money she had been saving for her daughters' future, and, with Irène's approval, using it to buy war bonds.

Marie was very much a French patriot during World War I, but she never forgot that she was a daughter of Poland. At the war's outbreak, she was distressed over the loss of communication with her family in Poland that the war had brought about. In a letter to Paul Langevin dated January 1, 1915, she wrote (as quoted in Eve's *Madame Curie*), "I am resolved to put all my strength at the service of my adopted country, since I cannot do anything for my unfortunate native country just now, bathed as it is in blood after more than a century of suffering." During the war, Polish nationalists succeeded in driving out the Russians. At the end of the war, in November 1918, Marie rejoiced not only in France's victory but also in the liberation of Poland. In 1919 an old friend from her early student days in Paris—pianist and composer Ignacy Jan Paderewski—became independent Poland's prime minister.

The famed classical pianist and postwar prime minister of Poland, Ignacy Jan Paderewski, was an old friend of Curie's, as this personally inscribed photograph attests.

Although the French government awarded Irène a military medal for her hospital work during the war, Marie received no official recognition. Perhaps her "adopted country" had not quite forgiven her for the Langevin affair.

Marie's war-related work continued for a period even after the war. Again in collaboration with Irène, she offered special radiology courses for a group of American soldiers who remained in France, awaiting evacuation orders, during the spring of 1919. She also spent that summer writing a book, *Radiology in War.* She took the opportunity to make a strong case for the benefits of basic research:

> The story of radiology in war offers a striking example of the unsuspected amplitude that the application of purely scientific discoveries can take under certain conditions.
>
> X rays had only a limited usefulness up to the time of the war. . . . A similar evolution took place in radiumtherapy, or the medical applications of radiations emitted by the radio elements.
>
> What are we to conclude from this unhoped-for development shared between the new radiations revealed to us by science at the end of the 19th century? It seems that they must make our confidence in disinterested research more alive and increase our reverence and admiration for it.

Over the years to come, Marie and her laboratory were to devote themselves to just such "disinterested research."

U.S. President Warren G. Harding escorts Curie to a White House reception given in her honor in 1921. Harding would present Curie with a most useful gift: a lead-lined mahogany box containing a gram of radium.

CHAPTER

8

"A Suitable Laboratory"

With the war over, Marie could now focus on realizing her long-term goal of developing, in Pierre's memory, what she hoped would be "a suitable laboratory." She already had a building, but she knew that she would need much more in order to create a world-class institution dedicated to the science of radioactivity.

The Radium Institute in 1919 had next to no equipment. Government support of science was inadequate. Money from the National Research Fund was barely enough to enable Marie to buy two measuring instruments. Private support for science was rare. To the extent that it existed, it was generally directed toward medical research. In 1920 Henri de Rothschild, a member of the wealthy philanthropic family, established the Curie Foundation to support some of the research done at the Radium Institute. But being a physician himself, Rothschild earmarked the foundation's funds for radiation therapy. None of the money went to support the physics and chemistry research done in Marie's part of the Institute.

Marie became "a laboratory patriot," as her daughter Eve described her in *Madame Curie*. The energy she had used to the country's benefit during the war was now focused on the laboratory. The same woman who for her entire teaching career of nearly three decades had suffered from stage fright before each lecture now developed the public relations skills to become a fund-raising phenomenon on her Institute's behalf.

In May 1920 Marie made the acquaintance of a woman without whose vision, driving force, and abilities the Radium Institute might never have amounted to much. It is not clear why she agreed to be interviewed by Mrs. William Brown Meloney, the editor of the *Delineator*, an American women's magazine. Marie remained hostile to journalists, whom she never forgave for destroying her personal happiness. The interview with Meloney, however, played a decisive role in determining the fortunes of the Radium Institute and in shaping Marie's role as a senior scientist.

As Meloney described the meeting in her introduction to Marie's *Pierre Curie,* the main emotion the interview aroused in her was shock when she compared the conditions under which the well-financed scientists in the United States worked, in well-equipped laboratories, with the labor of this "simple woman, working in an inadequate laboratory and living in an inexpensive apartment, on the meager pay of a French professor." Even greater was Meloney's discomfort when she learned that while the United States had about 50 grams of radium, the Institute run by the scientist who had discovered that element had only a single gram. Meloney asked Marie what she most fervently wished for. Marie's answer was simple: a second gram of radium for her laboratory.

Undeterred by the knowledge that a gram of radium cost about $100,000, almost overnight Meloney organized what she called the Marie Curie Radium Campaign to grant Marie's wish. Through her many contacts, she put together a committee of wealthy American women and distinguished American scientists willing to promote the cause and to encourage American citizens to contribute toward it. She arranged for the gram of radium that the campaign would buy to be handed to Marie at a White House reception given by the President of the United States himself. Meloney also arranged for an American publisher, the Macmillan Company, to publish Marie's biography of her husband, providing Marie with a source of royalty income over the years. *Pierre Curie* was published in November 1923.

Meloney's plan was based on the assumption that Marie would be willing to make a publicity tour of the United States. It was not easy for such a shy, private, and modest person to agree to this scheme of self-promotion, but Meloney was persuasive. Marie agreed to make the trip on one condition, that the American press must be muzzled. Not a word of the Langevin affair could appear in print. Meloney succeeded in charming promises out of every editor she approached, even editors of newspapers known for muckraking. From some she even managed to wheedle contributions to the Marie Curie Radium Fund, along with their pledge to suppress the Langevin story.

When it became known that President Warren G. Harding was going to honor Madame Curie personally, some French officials were embarrassed at France's failure to confer official distinction on her. The minister of public education tried to persuade Marie to accept the Legion of Honor, but she refused. She did, however, agree to attend a celebration to benefit the Radium Institute, held at the Paris Opéra on April 27, 1921, shortly before she set sail for the United States.

As Francoise Giroud quipped in her 1986 biography, *Marie Curie: A Life,* Marie "had to work almost as hard to extract the second gram of radium from the gold mine of America's spontaneous generosity as she had had to work to extract her first gram from the stubborn pitchblende." The tour Meloney had arranged for her was exhausting. Not many days into the trip, Marie's right hand had to be put in a sling to prevent it from being shaken further by overly enthusiastic well-wishers. The number of official events that Marie could attend had to be rethought. Luckily, both Eve and Irène had accompanied her on the trip, and one or the other often sub-

Curie meets the press as her boat docks in New York City in 1921. She overcame her aversion to publicity in order to gain access to the financial and scientific resources of the United States.

stituted for their mother at parties given by women who had donated large sums to the campaign. The tour, in fact, finally gave Eve a chance to shine. Unlike her mother and older sister, 16-year-old Eve actually enjoyed being charming in a social setting. More interested in jazz than in physics, Eve became a darling of hostesses and of the press, which dubbed her the girl "with the radium eyes."

In the course of her American tour, Marie was granted honorary degrees from Columbia, Yale, Chicago, and several other universities and women's colleges, including the University of Pennsylvania, Smith, and Wellesley. Harvard, however, did not grant Marie a degree. Some faculty members felt that her work was neither original nor independent and that she owed her success of two decades ago to her husband's guidance. (According to the university archives, Harvard did not grant an honorary degree to a woman until 1955, when Helen Keller became an honorary Doctor of Law.) Other American scientists also felt hostile to the fund-raising tour. Whatever money went to Marie's Radium Institute was money that might have gone to American laboratories.

This undercurrent of hostility, however, did not get in the way of the central event of the tour: the White House presentation, at which President Harding handed to Marie a mahogany box lined in lead, in which the radium would make the trip back to France. Marie dressed up for the occasion—she wore the same black dress she had worn to both Nobel ceremonies.

Among the honors Curie received while in the United States was an honorary doctorate of science bestowed upon her by Columbia University.

So successful was the Marie Curie Radium Campaign that much more went back to the Radium Institute than the single gram of radium. Marie also brought back other ores, a considerable amount of expensive equipment, and almost $7,000 in cash awards from different groups. In addition, over $50,000 remained in the Marie Curie Radium Fund in a New York bank. The interest from the account provided Marie an income for the rest of her life.

The success of the trip helped Marie to understand that as a 55-year-old scientist in charge of a research institution she must assume new responsibilities. The solitary life of a researcher that she had so much enjoyed in her younger days was no longer to be hers. She now understood the need to put up with public ceremonies. The good will and money they brought in could support the next generation of scientists at her institution. In 1929, she made a second trip to the United States, this time to benefit the Warsaw Radium Institute, founded four years earlier under her sister Bronya's directorship.

Marie was to turn the Radium Institute into an international center for the study of radioactivity. Its main rival was the Cavendish Laboratory in Cambridge, England, now under the direction of her friend Rutherford. Marie carefully selected a group of scientists, about 40 at a time, for the Institute's staff, always making sure to include some researchers from Poland and other foreign countries, as well as some women.

The young scientists at the Radium Institute began to make significant contributions. In 1929 Salomon Rosenblum made the first major discovery at the Curie laboratory. Using radioactive actinium that Marie herself had prepared for him, and a powerful electromagnet, he discovered that the alpha particles (helium nuclei) that were emitted did not all have exactly the same energy. Similar differences in energy in the light emitted by atoms had recently been interpreted using the new atomic theory known as quantum mechanics. Rosenblum's discovery thus implied that a similar analysis could reveal the internal structure of the nuclei that give off the alpha particles. This success was further scientific confirmation of the quantum theory.

Another young scientist at the Institute, Fernand Holweck, used a pump he designed himself to work out the details of the relationship between light and X rays. With his pump, he was able to create an especially high vacuum, enabling him to observe X rays of relatively long wavelength. Studies of these X rays clinched the identification of X rays as a form of radiation similar to light.

Bertrand Goldschmidt, a French chemist who served for a time as Marie Curie's personal assistant, later used techniques he learned at the Radium Institute to help the United States, the country in which he took refuge during World War II. Goldschmidt contributed to the development of the atomic bomb by extracting polonium from old radon tubes used by a New York cancer hospital. Marguerite Perey, another chemist at the Radium Institute, became known around the world in 1939 when she discovered the radioactive element francium while studying actinium.

Marie considered all her younger coworkers her children. Whenever any of them defended a thesis or received an award, Marie would treat the entire staff to a special tea. Cookies were served in darkroom developing dishes, and tea was brewed in flasks over Bunsen burners and poured into beakers to drink. But the most outstanding stars of the Radium Institute were her own child, Irène, and her son-in-law, Frédéric Joliot. Irène and Frédéric, who met at the Radium Institute, had a scientific collaboration similar to that of Marie and Pierre a generation earlier. On January 15, 1934, they announced their discovery that radioactive isotopes could be artificially created by bombarding the nuclei of certain elements with alpha particles. Just as Pierre and Marie used to make gifts of tubes of radium to their most esteemed colleagues, so Frédéric and Irène gave Marie a tube containing the first sample of an artificially created radioactive isotope. Thanks to the discovery of the Joliot-Curies, artificial radioactive isotopes could now be prepared relatively inexpensively, and the high cost and laborious work of separating naturally occurring radioactive elements from their ores would no longer slow down the development of nuclear physics.

Marie died less than half a year later. When Irène and Frédéric gave their lecture upon receiving the Nobel Prize for chemistry in December 1935, husband and wife were both on the podium and both spoke. At one point, Frédéric looked up from his prepared remarks and said, "It was certainly a satisfaction for our late lamented teacher, Marie Curie, to have seen the list of radioactive elements that she had the honor to inaugurate with Pierre Curie so extended."

Even though Marie devoted more energy in the last years of her life to administration and fund-raising than to her own scientific inquiries, she kept her hand in productive research until the end. In a letter she wrote to Bronya in September 1927, quoted by Eve in *Madame Curie*, Marie wrote, "Sometimes my courage fails me and I think I ought to stop

A family tradition: Irène Curie and her husband, Frédéric Joliot, receive the 1935 Nobel Prize for chemistry for their work on the artificial creation of radioactive isotopes.

working. . . . But I am held by a thousand bonds. . . . Nor do I know whether, even by writing scientific books, I could live without the laboratory." She also stayed informed about recent developments by going to scientific conferences. At the Solvay Congress of 1933 she was no longer the only woman in attendance. Her daughter Irène and the German physicist Lise Meitner (1878–1968) were also participants. Meitner's research would lead to the discovery that uranium nuclei can split into fragments, releasing enormous amounts of energy, in a process known as nuclear fission. Nuclear fission is the principle behind the atomic bomb.

Under Marie's guidance, from 1919 until her death in 1934, the chemists and physicists at the Radium Institute published 483 works, including 31 papers and books by Marie Curie herself. During the same period, the biomedical section of the Institute was similarly productive, treating over 8,000 patients. While Marie Curie did not participate in the medical research, she followed its progress with great interest.

But while medical issues were never more than a secondary interest to Marie Curie as a scientist, from 1920 on they became more and more central to her personal life. In that year, complaining of problems with her vision, Marie learned that she had a double cataract. Today it is known that this abnormality of the eye, in which the lens no longer lets light pass through, may be caused by prolonged exposure to radiation. Marie also began to suffer from tinnitus, a ringing in the ear. In a letter to Bronya on November 10, 1920, quoted by Eve in *Madame Curie,* she wrote, "Perhaps radium has something to do with these troubles, but it cannot be affirmed with certainty." She did her best to keep her loss of vision a secret, writing her lecture notes in enormous letters, and having her daughters shepherd her around from place to place. She eventually underwent four operations that succeeded in restoring her vision. During her periods of recuperation, her daughter Eve played the role of companion, thus strengthening the bond between them. As a result of medical treatment, Marie was able to do delicate laboratory work and to drive a car until the end of her life.

She continued, however, to ignore the growing evidence that overexposure to radiation can damage one's health and lead to an early death. One former Radium Institute researcher died in January 1925 of aplastic anemia, a blood disorder that can result from the toxic effects of radiation. A second chemist who had been Marie's personal assistant died of leukemia, another blood disease. Marie authorized a report to investigate the two deaths, but she implied in handwriting on the bottom margin of the final document that the scientists were responsible for their own deaths. They had let their

Two of the presiding scientific geniuses of the 20th century, Marie Curie and Albert Einstein, enjoy a quiet moment together in Geneva, Switzerland, in 1925.

exhaustion get the better of them, she believed, and had not taken sufficient exercise or fresh air in the last months of their lives. The Radium Institute continued to issue no warnings to incoming researchers. The only protective measure staff members took was to shield themselves from direct beams of radiation by using metal screens. Although each member of the staff was required to take a blood test at regular intervals, Marie herself rarely had her own blood count checked, though she sensed it was abnormal.

In early 1932 Marie slipped in the laboratory and broke her right wrist trying to steady herself. The break did not heal as quickly as it should have, and other distressing health problems intensified. The old radiation burns on her fingers began to hurt more. The tinnitus worsened. On some days she felt too ill to go to the laboratory. On those days she stayed home and worked on the book that would be published in 1935 under the title *Radioactivity.*

Although her death was not yet imminent, Marie began to prepare for it. Already while in the United States in 1921, she had asked Mrs. Meloney to take legal steps to ensure that the radium from the American tour remain the property of the Radium Institute after her death. Now she asked Meloney, who had become a close friend, to burn all the letters Marie had sent her over the past decade. Meloney only partially complied with this request.

When X rays taken in December 1933 revealed that Marie had a large gallstone, she was terrified. Her father had died of complications following a gallstone operation, and she refused to undergo a similar operation. Instead, she put herself on a strict diet and was soon back at the lab. To prove how healthy she was, she joined Irène and Frédéric on a skiing holiday in the Alps. One evening she was late in joining them in their chalet, and the couple began to fear the worst. But Marie soon returned, full of excitement. She had gone off on snowshoes to see a magnificent sunset on Mont Blanc, the Alps' highest peak.

By the time of her next holiday at Easter in 1934, Marie had taken a definite turn for the worse. Her sister Bronya joined her for a trip to Provence in the south of France. Before leaving, Marie went through her own files and destroyed many documents. She also told Irène that she was leaving instructions about the American radium together with other documents that could, if need be, serve as a will. In the course of the trip, the sisters stopped to visit Jacques Curie. Neither her sister nor her brother-in-law would see Marie alive again.

Marie returned from the trip in the grip of a fever. Not long afterward, one day in mid-May, Marie, feeling very ill, left the laboratory and went home at 3:30 in the afternoon. On her way, she stopped to ask the caretaker to attend to a rosebush that was doing poorly. She never returned to the Radium Institute.

Despite all her medical problems, Marie had no personal physician. None of the specialists she saw ever charged her for services rendered, and Marie hated to take advantage of them.

But not even the director of biomedical research at the Radium Institute, who visited Marie at home, could diagnose her current problem. Four distinguished physicians whom Eve insisted she visit suggested that it might be tuberculosis, and so Eve took her mother on a long and physically demanding trip to a sanatorium. However, X rays taken there showed that her lungs were unaffected and that the difficult journey to the mountains had been in vain. In despair, Eve summoned a medical professor from Geneva, who identified the problem and indicated that there was no cure. Marie was suffering from aplastic anemia, the same blood disorder that had killed her former coworker in 1925.

The director of the sanatorium released the news of Marie's death on July 4, 1934. That day marked the end of one era and the beginning of a new one. Before her realization that radioactivity was an atomic property, scientists believed that the atom was unchangeable. Once scientists began to develop the science of radioactivity, they learned about the vast energy contained within the atomic nucleus. On July 4, 1934, Marie Curie lay on her deathbed. On that day, too, according to Richard Rhodes in *The Making of the Atomic Bomb,* Leo Szilard, a physicist born in Hungary in 1898 (the year Marie Curie discovered polonium and radium), filed a patent describing a device that could produce an explosion by releasing the energy inside the atom. Some years later in the United States, Szilard helped conduct the first sustained nuclear chain reaction, which would lead to the development of the atomic bomb.

On July 6, 1934, Marie Curie was buried in the same cemetery in Sceaux where she had seen the burial of her mother-in-law, her husband, and her father-in-law. Her sister and brother came from Warsaw, bringing with them some Polish soil, which they threw into the open grave. Over 60 years later, on April 20, 1995, the remains of Pierre and Marie Curie were transferred from the tomb in Sceaux to the Panthéon, France's national mausoleum, in Paris. Marie Curie thus became the first woman to be accorded, on the basis of her own accomplishments, the honor of being buried along-side France's most eminent men.

Marie Curie left behind no written testament revealing how well she felt she had lived up to her youthful aspiration of developing herself and contributing to the welfare of others. But there was no doubt about her accomplishments in the minds of two of the major physicists of the 20th century, Ernest Rutherford and Albert Einstein. Both of these distinguished friends and colleagues published a eulogy on the occasion of Marie Curie's death. Rutherford's tribute took the form of an obituary in the British scientific journal *Nature*. He wrote:

> Madame Curie . . . held an outstanding position in science, for she had long been regarded as the foremost woman investigator of our age. . . . The discovery and isolation of radium was an event of outstanding significance to science from both the theoretical and practical points of view. . . . [Radium] has . . . played an important part in the growth of our knowledge of the internal structure of atoms in general. In addition, radium . . . has proved an invaluable adjunct in the treatment of cancerous growths. . . . The many friends of Madame Curie around the world, who admired her not only for her scientific talents but also for her fine character and personality, lament the untimely removal of one who had made such great contributions to knowledge, and, through her discoveries, to the welfare of mankind.

For his part, Einstein in 1935 published "Marie Curie in Memoriam." He praised her for acting on the conviction that she was always "a servant of society." He attributed her discovery of radium and polonium "not merely to bold intuition but to a devotion and tenacity in execution under the most extreme hardships imaginable."

But the first woman to win a Nobel Prize, the first individual to win two Nobel Prizes, and the first Nobel Prize winner to have a child win another Nobel Prize might have been most pleased with another of Einstein's judgments: "Marie Curie is, of all celebrated beings, the only one whom fame has not corrupted."

CHRONOLOGY

November 7, 1867
Marie Sklodowska is born in Warsaw, Poland

November 5, 1891
Marie Sklodowska registers as a student at the Sorbonne

July 26, 1895
Marie Sklodowska marries Pierre Curie

September 12, 1897
Irène Curie is born

April 12, 1898
Marie Curie introduces the term radioactivity in a published article

July 18, 1898
Pierre and Marie Curie announce the discovery of polonium

July 26, 1898
Pierre Curie, Marie Curie, and Gustave Bémont announce the discovery of radium

December 1903
Henri Becquerel, Pierre Curie, and Marie Curie share the Nobel Prize for physics for their work on radioactivity

December 6, 1904
Eve Curie is born

April 19, 1906
Marie Curie becomes a widow when Pierre Curie dies in an accident

November 5, 1906

Marie Curie becomes the first woman professor at the Sorbonne

December 1911

Marie Curie is awarded the Nobel Prize for chemistry for discovering radium and polonium and for isolating radium, thus becoming the first person to receive two Nobel Prizes

August 1914

Construction of the Radium Institute is completed just after the outbreak of World War I

1914–1919

Marie Curie runs a radiology service and introduces radon therapy to France

May–June 1921

Marie Curie travels to the United States to receive a gram of radium donated by the American people to the Radium Institute

January 15, 1934

Irène and Frédéric Joliot-Curie announce their discovery of artificial radioactivity

July 4, 1934

Marie Curie dies, at the age of 66, of aplastic anemia

April 20, 1995

Marie Curie is reburied in the Panthéon, France's national mausoleum, becoming the first woman accorded that honor on her own merit

FURTHER READING

Autobiography

Curie, Marie. *Pierre Curie*. Translated by Charlotte and Vernon Kellogg. New York: Macmillan, 1932. (Marie Curie's *Autobiographical Notes* are included at the end of *Pierre Curie*.)

Biographies

Birch, Beverley. *Marie Curie: Pioneer in the Study of Radiation.* Milwaukee: Gareth Stevens, 1988.

Bull, Angela. *Marie Curie*. London: Hamish Hamilton, 1986.

Curie, Eve. *Madame Curie*. Translated by Vincent Sheean. 1937. Reprint. New York: Da Capo, 1986.

Giroud, Francoise. *Marie Curie: A Life*. Translated by Lydia Davis. New York: Holmes & Meier, 1986.

Jaffe, Bernard, "Curie: The Story of Marie and Pierre," in *Crucibles: The Story of Chemistry*. New York: Dover, 1976.

Keller, Mollie. *Marie Curie*. New York: Franklin Watts, 1982.

Magill, Frank N., ed. "Pierre and Marie Curie, 1903," in *The Nobel Prize Winners: Physics,* vol. 1. Pasadena, Calif., and Englewood Cliffs, New Jersey: Salem Press, 1989.

———, ed. "Marie Curie, 1911," in *The Nobel Prize Winners: Chemistry,* vol. 1. Pasadena, California, and Englewood Cliffs, New Jersey: Salem Press, 1990.

McGrayne, Sharon Bertsch. "Marie Sklodowska Curie," in *Nobel Prize Women in Science: Their Lives, Struggles, and Momentous Discoveries*. New York: Birch Lane Press, 1993.

Opfell, Olga S. *The Lady Laureates: Women Who Have Won the Nobel Prize*. Metuchen, New Jersey: Scarecrow Press, 1986.

Pflaum, Rosalynd. *Grand Obsession: Madame Curie and Her World*. New York: Doubleday, 1989.

———. *Marie Curie and Her Daughter Irène*. Minneapolis: Lerner, 1993.

Quinn, Susan. *Marie Curie: A Life*. New York: Simon & Schuster, 1995.

Reid, Robert William. *Marie Curie.* New York: New American Library, 1978.

Woznicki, Robert. *Madame Curie—Daughter of Poland.* Miami: American Institute of Polish Culture, 1983.

Books Containing Selections from the Writings of Marie Curie

Romer, Alfred, ed. "The Curies: Polonium and Radium," in *Radiochemistry and the Discovery of Isotopes.* New York: Dover, 1970.

Weaver, Jefferson Hane, ed. "Radioactivity," in *The World of Physics.* New York: Simon & Schuster, 1987.

Books about Physics and Other Physicists

Clark, Ronald W. *Einstein: The Life and Times.* New York: World, 1971.

French, A. P., ed. *Einstein: A Centenary Volume.* Cambridge: Harvard University Press, 1979.

Pais, Abraham. *Subtle Is the Lord...: The Science and the Life of Albert Einstein.* New York: Oxford University Press, 1982.

Rhodes, Richard. *The Making of the Atomic Bomb.* New York: Simon & Schuster, 1986.

Rossiter, Margaret W. *Women Scientists in America: Struggles and Strategies to 1940.* Baltimore: Johns Hopkins University Press, 1982.

Segrè, Emilio. *From X-Rays to Quarks: Modern Physicists and Their Discoveries.* San Francisco: Freeman, 1980.

Weart, Spencer R. *Scientists in Power.* Cambridge: Harvard University Press, 1979.

ACKNOWLEDGMENTS

A number of individuals played a variety of roles in helping this book come to be. First I wish to thank Professor Owen Gingerich of Harvard University and Nancy Toff of Oxford University Press for inviting me to participate in this series of scientific biographies for young adults. Thanks to their invitation I was privileged to experience a feeling hitherto unknown to me: the compulsion to leap out of bed early each morning so that I could find out what I had to say about this fascinating woman scientist in whose life I had become so immersed.

I am grateful to Mrs. Henry R. Labouisse of New York City, née Eve Curie, not only for her stimulating classic biography of her mother but also for permission to quote from her book, *Madame Curie,* as well as from her mother's book, *Pierre Curie.*

Through the technological wonder of e-mail, my Parisian friends Franck Laloë of the Ecole Normale Supérieure (ENS) and Suzanne Laloë of the Institut d'Astrophysique put me in touch with helpful contacts at the Institut Curie. The Laloës also assisted me in shaping a phrase summarizing the importance of the ENS in the French academic hierarchy. Also from Paris, but via snail mail, Mme Monique Bordry and Mme Ginette Gablot of the Musée Curie were kind enough to send impressive documents describing current research activities at the Institut Curie.

Professor Raymond Chang of Williams College sent me an important bibliographic reference that helped me understand and evaluate Mme Curie's thesis research. Professor Marek Demianski, also at Williams College in 1993-1994, while on leave from the Copernicus Astronomical Institute in Warsaw, was kind enough to take and send me photographs of Polish sites related to Mme Curie.

None of these individuals, of course, is to blame for whatever errors of fact or interpretation may remain in my book, for which I alone take responsibility.

Finally I wish to thank members of my family for their support over the years and during the development of this project. My parents, Anna Jacobson Schwartz and Isaac Schwartz, have played as significant a role in shaping my attitude toward the value of work as Marie Curie's parents played in hers. My husband, Jay M. Pasachoff, and my daughters, Eloise and Deborah Pasachoff, cheerfully tolerated my months-long obsession with Marie Curie and helped edit the first draft. I am eternally grateful to these family members.

Naomi Pasachoff, a research associate at Williams College, is the co-author of several school and college science textbooks and author of a variety of other textbooks and trade books. She has taught English composition and literature at Williams College, Rensselaer Polytechnic Institute, and Skidmore College. She holds an A.B. from Radcliffe College, Harvard University, an A.M. from Columbia University, and a Ph.D. from Brandeis University.

Owen Gingerich is a senior astronomer at the Smithsonian Astrophysical Observatory and Professor of Astronomy and of the History of Science at Harvard University. He has served as vice president of the American Philosophical Society and as chairman of the U.S. National Committee of the International Astronomical Union. The author of more than 400 articles and reviews, Professor Gingerich is also the author of *The Great Copernicus Chase and Other Adventures in Astronomical History,* and *The Eye of Heaven: Ptolemy, Copernicus, Kepler.* The International Astronomical Union's Minor Planet Bureau has named Asteroid 2658 "Gingerich" in his honor.